Big Dreams in Small Places
Church Planting in Smaller Communities

Dr. Thomas P. Nebel

D0012792

St. Charles, IL 60174
1-800-253-4276

Published by ChurchSmart Resources

We are an evangelical Christian publisher committed to producing excellent products at affordable prices to help church leaders accomplish effective ministry in the areas of church planting, church growth, church renewal and leadership development.

For a free catalog of our resources call 1-800-253-4276.

Cover design by: Julie Becker
Manuscript edited by: Kim Miller and Peggy Newell

ISBN#: 889638-28-5

Dedication

"To Mike Ball, who from rural anonymity
has a vision to change the world."

Big Dreams in Small Places

Church Planting in Smaller Communities

CONTENTS

FOREWORD: BY DR. ROBERT E. LOGAN

From the first time I met Tom, he had a heart for church planting. In 1985 I was speaking at a chapel service at Denver Seminary, where he was a student. God gave him such a vision for church planting at that service that he went straight from the chapel to the phone, called his wife and said, "I know what we're supposed to do with the rest of our lives."

Shortly afterwards Tom set up an appointment with me and told me, "I know I'm supposed to do church planting." As I began asking him some questions about his background, I discovered his family had been in Wisconsin for five or six generations, as had his wife's family. I looked at him and said, "Well, you're so equipped and prepared to work within that culture that there's really only one place for you to go. Go back to Wisconsin." So he went to Whitewater, Wisconsin, a small college town of about 6,000 permanent residents, and planted a church there. Soon afterwards, a daughter church was born in neighboring Oconomowoc. Then another, and another.

Three things are necessary for successful church planting and multiplication: the right person, the right place, and the right plan. Many people ask me, "Where are there growing communities where I can plant?" But that's not the right question. The question we need to ask is, "Where are there unreached people that I am equipped to reach?" In fact, many denominations start their movements in the most resistant areas. If they included smaller communities in their thinking, they might gain the momentum necessary to impact the more difficult areas as well.

So often we get wrapped up in the American success syndrome: bigger is better. Instead, we are called to develop a harvest orientation—and much of the harvest is found in smaller towns. We need to make plans for reaching the entire harvest, all segments of society.

Some planters who may not succeed in big cities could flourish in the right place. People can have a phenomenal degree of effectiveness when they find that perfect fit, the place and the people that are the right match for them. For those who find that match in smaller towns, *Big Dreams in Small Places* is a must read. The book is packed with wisdom and insight that will help inform strategy. In order to do effective ministry in small communities, certain cultural dynamics must be understood. Tom's insights, as he unpacks the uniqueness of small town culture, will have a huge impact on a harvest that's often overlooked.

The principles Tom sets forth in *Big Dreams in Small Places* are based on solid research and experience. The book flows out of his doctoral dissertation, for which I served as a mentor. Tom knows how to apply proven church planting principles in the unique context of smaller communities. *Big Dreams in Small Places* is a much-needed resource in the church planting field.

INTRODUCTION:

Well I was born in a small town
And I live in a small town
Prob'ly die in a small town
Oh, those small communities

All my friends are so small town
My parents live in the same small town
My job is so small town
Provides little opportunity

Educated in a small town
Taught the fear of Jesus in a small town
Used to daydream in that small town
Another boring romantic that's me[1]

Rock and roller John Mellencamp grew up in small town Indiana, and he thought enough of his heritage to put his experience to music. It's a place of tradition, relatives, and friends. If you grew up in a small town you know there's a magnetic pull that keeps bringing you back. You never do get it out of your system, even when you're a big-time recording artist.

For millions of Americans small towns are places to live, work, make friends, raise their families, and die. And some are "taught the fear of Jesus" there, too. Ask urbanites to describe a small town and they'll likely miss the mark. They'll either spout a romantic image of Andy Griffith and Barney Fife in Mayberry, or they'll give you the tired cliché of a rusted out Midwestern hick town with Mama pulling the wash off the clothesline. Sure, those extremes exist, but most small communities are typical, secure, progressive, wonderful, vibrant, healthy—and needy. Somewhere in the middle lies a huge mission field that is ripe for a relevant gospel witness.

My wife, Lori, and I grew up in a small town, too, in northeast Wisconsin. Sturgeon Bay, with a population of 9,000 or so, was a great

---

[1]John Mellencamp, "Small Town," *Scarecrow*, Mercury Records, 1985.

place to call home. It was known both for its shipbuilding industry and
for its tourism, as the gateway to one of the Midwest's primary
playgrounds, the Door County Peninsula. My family lived its life within a
span of three miles. There was our home, which was built by my great-
grandfather, on 4th Avenue. My dad was born in that house, and he died
there, too. The family business, Nebel Electric, was a few blocks south,
on 3rd Avenue. It was founded by my grandfather in 1903. To the north,
just a couple of miles down Bayshore Drive, was the family cottage with
its big sand beach on the bay where we had all of our fun and made most
of our memories.

> No I cannot forget where it is that I come from
> I cannot forget the people who love me
> Yeah, I can be myself here in this small town
> And people let me be just what I want to be
> Got nothing against a big town
> Still hayseed enough to say
> Look who's in the big town
> But my bed is in a small town
> Oh, and that's good enough for me[2]

For most of my adult life I've lived in metropolitan areas but that
changed in August 2002. We're now participants in the "rural rebound",
having felt the pull back to a smaller community. Part of it is sentiment,
to be sure. "I cannot forget where it is that I come from, I cannot forget
the people who love me." But that's not the entire reason. The main
reason for the pull is that I was "taught the fear of Jesus in a small town,"
and if someone hadn't planted a church there thirty years earlier I
wonder if I ever would have found the Savior.

The fact that Lori and I found Jesus in a small town eventually
propelled us to become church planters, too. We planted a church in
another small town in Wisconsin where hundreds of others found Him.
Our church in Whitewater reproduced itself several times in other small
communities with wonderful results. The experience got me thinking
about other small towns and rural areas across North America that have
been neglected by denominations and church planters who could reach
so many people—and build reproducing church planting movements in
the process. So I initiated a movement of new churches across my state
in which nearly forty small town churches have been planted over the last
eight years. Most have grown to vibrancy and are, with the evident
blessing of God, fulfilling the Great Commission in their areas.

[2]Ibid.

In this book I'll address a number of issues related to planting churches in smaller markets, and in the process I hope to help 1) church planters who will plant the small town or rural church, and 2) denominational representatives who are responsible to engineer church planting movements in their regions.

I'll make the case that we have a responsibility to plant churches in small towns and rural areas and that "small town" doesn't need to mean "small church." I'll show that small towns are easier places to plant new churches than most other areas. And I'll demonstrate that these places, near to the heart of God, provide excellent launching pads to forge reproducing church planting movements that reach all kinds of communities, large and small.

Tom Nebel
Madison, Wis.

PART ONE: GOD'S PLAN FOR SMALL COMMUNITIES

Chapter 1: Capitalizing on America's Rural Rebound

BIG NEWS ABOUT SMALL TOWNS

You probably already know that God cares about church planting and that he cares about all kinds of people in all kinds of settings worldwide. You know that churches die and that we're way behind in the us/them Great Commission battle. And you probably can quote missiologist C. Peter Wagner who said that the planting of healthy new churches is "the best evangelistic method under heaven." So why the emphasis here on the smaller market? To begin, there are some serious demographic realities to consider.

Not everyone lives in a big city. In fact, Americans are moving to small towns, and those in the popular media are taking note. In a recent lead article in the Life section of *USA Today* writer Wanda Urbanska remarks on just that reality. "The yearning is there . . . we grew up emotional and geographical transients. . . . We're looking to put our roots down (by moving to small towns). . . ."[3] The trend is noted by Loyola University demographer Kenneth Johnson, who refers to this phenomenon as "the Rural Rebound." According to Johnson, rural America lost 1.4 million people in the 1980s to urban and suburban areas, but more than 1.8 million people have reversed those numbers in the nineties and the first decade of the twenty-first century by moving to smaller towns.[4] The cover story of the December 8, 1997 issue of *Time* magazine leads with "Why More Americans are Fleeing to Small Towns," where the figures are deemed to be even larger.

---

[3]Wanda Urbanska, "Boomers Bewitched by Charms of Small Towns," *USA Today*, 22 April, 1997, D-1.
[4]Ibid, 1-2.

A new kind of 'white flight' is going on in America today, but unlike the middle-class exodus from multiethnic cities to the suburbs a generation ago, this middle-class migration is from crowded, predominantly white suburbs to small towns and rural counties. Rural America has enjoyed a net inflow of 2 million Americans this decade—that is, 2 million more people have moved from metropolitan centers to rural areas than have gone the traditional small-town-to-big-city route. Thanks to the newcomers, 75% of the nation's rural counties are growing again after years of decline. Some towns are even booming, with high-tech industrial parks and bustling downtowns in which refurbished storefronts boast serious restaurants and community theaters, ubiquitous brew pubs and coffee bars."[5]

Add to this the stack of recent popular books either referencing the new migration or romanticizing small town life, and it is clear that small towns, to many, are no longer the overlooked and under appreciated municipalities they once were. Ron Klassen and John Koesler in their book, *No Little Places*, affirm what others are saying. "During a recent ten-year period, U.S. towns of twenty-five hundred or less in nonurban areas grew by 4.9 percent. Twenty-five percent of all Americans live in these towns."[6]

What is a small town? Not everyone agrees on the definition, and a lot depends on personal perspective and experience. I grew up in Sturgeon Bay, Wis., a community of 9,000 people. When we would go to the "big city" we had Green Bay (population today: 100,000) in mind. Yet, as a committed follower of the National Football League, I am always unnerved when I hear Green Bay, home of the Packers, referred to in the national media as a small town. Sure, Green Bay is the smallest community in the United States to host a major level sports franchise, but it's not really a small town. Some demographers call a small town anything under 50,000, and some would say much less than that. Not even the United States Census Bureau has a clear definition.

Add to this the fact that "some urbanites use the terms 'small town' and 'country' interchangeably"[7] and we have a new set of definitions to think through. Our definitions depend on our perspective, and my own experience bears this out. While planting a church in Whitewater, Wis., I was referenced by my friend, church growth and church planting leader Bob Logan, a Los Angeles native, in *Beyond Church Growth* along the same lines. "Tom Nebel discovered that in the *rural* community of Whitewater, Wisconsin. . . ."[8] But Whitewater had nearly 12,000 residents,

[5](author), "Why More Americans are Fleeing to Small Towns," *Time*, 8 December 1997, 54.
[6]Ron Klassen and John Koessler, *No Little Places* (Grand Rapids: Baker, 1996), 57-58.
[7]John Clayton, *Small Town Bound* (Franklin Lakes, NJ: Career Press, 1996), 14.
[8]Robert E. Logan, *Beyond Church Growth* (Old Tappan, NJ: Revell, 1989), 69.

including university students. To me, "rural" has always meant "on the farm." I was living in a small town.

With no other agreed-upon definition of small town to direct my thinking I will define a small town as a community with the following characteristics:

- a population base (not including rural population which would orient toward the community) between 2,500 and 15,000;

- the community stands alone; it is not attached to or dependent upon a metropolis as a bedroom community or as a suburb.

The Rural Rebound that we currently experience is occurring for a number of reasons. In his book, *Small Town Bound*, John Clayton sets the stage:

> Everything about this migration is new, not just the direction. In fact, if you're part of it, you're part of one of the hottest demographic trends in the country. In analyzing the trend, sociologists have pointed out two unique factors. The first is motivation. In the past, people moved from rural areas to cities to improve their economic or cultural opportunities. Or they moved from one metropolitan area to another . . . because of the demands of a career. But today, people are moving away from the cities for a host of other, interconnected reasons. These reasons are frequently summed up in the phrase "quality of life." . . .
>
> The second unique factor is the demographic diversity of the new migrants. It used to be that young people left rural areas to start life in the city. But the faces of migration are changing. . . .[9]

It's true: the faces of migration are changing. First, there are the burned-out professionals who have tired of the rat race of urban living. A classic example is Marilyn Abraham, a powerful executive with publisher Simon & Schuster, and her husband Sandy MacGregor. They had the world by the tail, living a glamorous lifestyle and owning both a fashionable Manhattan apartment and a home in the country. But a series of friends' deaths and personal exhaustion triggered their decision to "get out." Her book, *First We Quit Our Jobs: How One Work-Driven Couple Got on the Road to a New Life*, chronicles how they drove their recreational vehicle for four months across North America and eventually settled in a small town in the vicinity of Santa Fe, New Mexico Abraham reflects:

---

[9]Clayton, *Small Town Bound*, 12.

We had difficulty getting people to believe, and at the same time reinforcing to ourselves, that we really really really had been thoroughly and deeply happy in that $35,000, 240-square-foot motor home. Living in it might not be the exact way we wanted to spend the rest of our lives (maybe it was?), but it made crystal clear the fact that the alternative—working crazy hours to support a house we had very little time to be in—wasn't the design for the future. He who dies with the most toys is still dead, no?[10]

Besides burned-out urbanites, the Rural Rebound now consists of a sizable number of retirees. These senior citizens, who may live between one-fourth and one-third of their lives in retirement, now have the opportunity to live for many years anywhere they desire. The small town idea has appealed to many of them for some time, but only now can their emigration fantasy become a reality. Many retirees will fulfill their dream by considering such factors as weather, leisure-time activities, clean air and water, and the perceived friendliness of a small town.

Another Rural Rebound migrant may be referred to as the "modem cowboy"—a professional who may move to a smaller town or rural area because modern technology allows him or her to relocate without hindrance to business. Not too many years ago such workers or entrepreneurs would have necessarily been anchored to a given location, where business contacts and customers were located. However, with the advent of electronic mail, the Internet, faxes, and the other advantages of the communication age, mobility is possible for many today.

Finally, there are those who move for all the reasons that others move, including work. When business owners decide to move operations to a smaller community or rural area, others (blue-collars, retailers, salesman, and so on) are necessarily affected. As an example, Cray Supercomputers, a leader in mainframe computer manufacturing, moved its operation from Minneapolis to Chippewa Falls, Wis. (population 13,000). A personal friend of mine moved their manufacturing business from Chicago to scenic Door County, Wis. "because we always vacationed there and decided we could live there year-round."

The Rural Rebound is occurring because people believe a better life awaits them on the other side. The Gallup Organization recently asked Americans to state their preferred community in which to live. The result was that 19 percent preferred the city, 22 percent a farm, 24 percent a suburb, and 34 percent a small town.[11] Marilyn and Tom Ross, in their guide to entrepreneurs who may wish to relocate, *Country Bound!*, list a number of factors, all of which relate to personal freedom and fulfillment.

---

[10]Marilyn Abraham, *First We Quit Our Jobs* (New York: Dell, 1997), 230.
[11]Clayton, *Small Town Bound*, 59.

Americans are searching. We're looking for answers. Our senses are assaulted, our energy invaded, our peace of mind threatened. The culprit? Big City Stress. . . . If you feel unsettled, exploited, stifled— journey with us in exploring a new option. It may not be the right path for you. On the other hand, it may offer a pilgrimage to freedom. Freedom is, after all, a matter of choice.[12]

Many people at least have a favorable impression of small towns and small town living. There are a number of perceived advantages these communities hold in the hearts of Americans, including:

- The notion of rediscovering our roots. There is a longing for community within all people that is often not fulfilled in an urban lifestyle.

- The ability to feel safe and secure. Sure there is crime, and there are difficulties, but "gang wars and drive-by shootings are foreign concepts in Small Town USA."[13] In the wake of terrorist threats in the United States, people may find the allure of small town living too strong to pass up.

- The enjoyment of a true quality of life. This catchall phrase can refer to pollution, noise, and mortality. "Cancer incidence is 6 percent higher in urban areas. . . ."[14]

- The reduction of stress. No long commutes, traffic jams, and so on.

- The lowering of the cost of living. Housing prices, taxes, utilities, repair/maintenance, insurance and other related issues are often significantly cheaper in a smaller town.

- Finding a favorable climate. Climate includes water, elevation, and wind. The move to a smaller community may coincide with a favorable climate change.

- Enjoying health and wellness. In addition to health matters referenced above, *Psychology Today* reports that smaller communities provide the conditions necessary for sound mental health.[15]

- Putting leisure back in life. Sports participation (both for adults and children) and other recreation activities are often more readily available.

With these demographic and sociological realities, you'd think that we'd be lining up to plant churches in these places. In some cases we are, but in some ways we're overlooking an incredible harvest field.

---

[12]Marilyn Ross and Tom Ross, *Country Bound!* (Chicago: Upstart Publications, 1997), 14.
[13]Ibid., 16.
[14]Ibid., 18.
[15]Ibid., 57.

THE CURRENT BIAS TOWARD
URBAN AND SUBURBAN CENTERS

When I first considered church planting as a ministry in 1984 there were very few resources (books, tapes, conferences, and so on) available to pastors or church planters who were seeking church growth or church planting information. I eagerly devoured what little was available. Though some of what I read was helpful, and though my knowledge base was limited, I intuitively started to observe a pattern. It seemed as though, by implication, the authors of church planting and church growth resources were suggesting that the best places, if not the only places, where God could start and grow churches were in growing urban and suburban environments. I was glad for any information on environment, but I did recoil a bit, observing to my wife that "if this stuff was from God we should be able to apply it in stable population bases, such as in our home state of Wisconsin." That realization entered into our decision-making process, and we ended up returning to our roots.

Church growth literature has made significant strides since that time, and the Christian world is blessed with a plethora of information and agencies that give strategic aid to kingdom-expanding ventures. This is good, helpful, and necessary. Having said that, the preponderance of information today shows a strong bias toward the city and urban ventures. Prayer strategist Ed Silvoso exemplifies this in his book *That None Should Perish* by stating "Cities are central to God's redemptive strategy. The Great Commission begins with a city—Jerusalem—and culminates when another city—the new Jerusalem—becomes God's eternal dwelling with His people."[16] Yes, let's care for and emphasize the city, but I doubt that Silvoso makes a convincing theological argument here. I could easily quote the Gospel of Mark: "Jesus replied, 'Let us go somewhere else—to the nearby villages—so I can preach there also. That is why I have come" (Mark 1:38, NIV). Couldn't it just as easily be said, "Small towns are central to God's redemptive strategy. Jesus was born in a small town, and he was raised in a small town, and said it was his purpose to go to small towns . . ."? As a further example of contemporary church growth bias, consider John Dawson's *Taking Our Cities for God:*

> Cities are simply huge clusters of people, and Jesus goes where the people are. In His earthly ministry Jesus wept with compassion for the crowds of Jersualem and moved among them in ministry.
>
> Over one-half of the world's population lives in urban centers. In developed nations like the United States, the percentage of urban

[16]Edward Silvoso, *That None Should Perish* (Ventura, Calif.: Regal Books, 1994), 21.

dwellers is much higher. In California, for example, 91 percent of the population lives in cities.

My city, Los Angeles, is crowded, expensive, violent and polluted. I would rather raise my children in rural isolation or suburban convenience, but Jesus has called me here. Jesus has always been attracted to the dark places. . . . By the year 2010, three out of every four people on earth will live in cities[17]

Dawson raises some good issues, and, for the record, I am a big fan of urban and suburban church planting. I lead a movement that plants many churches in such places. Nevertheless, some strategists, in their passion for the city, overlook other needy, dark areas where, by any reckoning, huge numbers of people live: small towns and rural areas. Just because some perceive "rural isolation" as "easier places to live" does not mean that we neglect such areas for the cause of Christ.

There is at least one exception in current thought when it comes to acknowledging the evangelization of smaller communities. Jim Montgomery, in his DAWN (disciple a whole nation) strategy shows the need for at least 7 million new churches across the globe. He makes a compelling argument that specific church planting goals are required in order to truly "reach" an area. Montgomery says that a group of people has been evangelized when there is: "1) an active, witnessing cell of believers in every village, town, urban neighborhood and ethnic community in the country; 2) a church for every geographical group of 300 to 1,000 people; 3) a viable church within geographical and socio-cultural reach of everyone."[18] This sort of logic can be scary or at least demoralizing because it reminds us how far we have to go. But his research is a sober reminder of the global realities should we seek "to have at least one . . . congregation in every village and city neighborhood, for every class, kind and condition of people in the world."

Upon occasion other books, such as Klassen and Koessler's *No Little Places: The Untapped Potential of the Small-Town Church* give some tribute to smaller communities. This is a fine book that serves as an apologetic for pastoral service in rural communities, but it is not a clarion call for forceful evangelism through the strategic establishment of new congregations. Consequently, the subtle implication is that "small town church" equates with "small church." I think that's a common stereotype. Most people, when asked to depict a small town church, will describe a single cell church of fewer than seventy people, mostly old and gray, and inhabiting a little white building with pews and a nice steeple on top. As you'll see, that's not the type of church I'm thinking of here.

[17]John Dawson, *Taking Our Cities for God* (Altamonte Springs, Fla.: Creation House, 1989), 34.
[18]James Montgomery, *DAWN 2000* (Pasadena, Calif.: William Carey Library, 1989), 49.

The urban and suburban bias in church growth and planting literature is reflected in the statistics. I conducted a nonscientific survey of the thirteen districts of my denomination, the Baptist General Conference, to compare the relative numbers of churches planted in rural/small town (populations fewer than 15,000), suburban, and urban environments over a recent five-year period. The result of this cursory survey, appearing in table 1, makes my point. Only 15 percent of all new church attempts were made in smaller towns or rural areas. The statistics are even more compelling when the data from the district where I served (Great Lakes) is eliminated from the survey. In that case, only 8 percent of new church attempts were made in small towns or rural areas (with urban plants attempted 30 percent of the time and suburban plants attempted 62 percent of the time). In other words, without an intentional regional strategy which

TABLE 1: CHURCH PLANT ATTEMPTS 1993-1997
According to Population in the Baptist General Conference

District	# of Urban Plants Plants Attempted	# of Suburban Plants Attempted	# of Small Town/Rural Plants Attempted
A	2	6	0
B	0	7	0
C	7	10	14
D	3	2	0
E	2	1	0
F	1	0	2
G	2	10	1
H	0	5	0
I	7	7	2
J	3	3	0
K	6	14	3
L	4	8	1
M	6	11	0
Totals (%)	43 (29%)	84 (56%)	23 (15%)

includes the planting of churches in small towns or rural areas, the likelihood in my denomination that a church will be planted in such a place is less than 10 percent. It appears that districts responsible for the planting of new churches in their area will naturally default to suburban church planting, will secondarily include urban church planting in their strategy, and then, perhaps as an afterthought, will include smaller towns. To be sure, some parts of our country consist primarily of small towns and rural areas, making them more natural targets for the planting of those types of churches. Additionally, the cultural roots of the Baptist General Conference are small town, rural, and agrarian—meaning that many smaller communities already have an established church representing the denomination. However, each region of the country has many smaller communities without an adequate gospel witness, so the neglect of these places cannot be simply assigned to market need. The truth is that many denominations, like my own, overlook the places of smaller populations in their church planting mission.

THE MOST COMPELLING REASON TO TARGET SMALL TOWNS

There is a vast and growing need for the planting of thousands of healthy new churches across the United States, not only in urban and suburban areas, but in small towns and rural regions as well. The current Rural Rebound migration suggests that we are approaching never-before-seen opportunities. But even if this weren't true, even if small towns across America were dustbins of antiquity with ever shrinking populations, there would still be a powerful reason to prioritize the planting of new churches in small towns and rural areas: the human reality that lives will be redeemed for eternity when people respond to the gospel.

In 1945 a young student from Bethel Seminary in St. Paul, Minn. traveled each weekend to a small community in northeast Wisconsin to attempt to start a new church. The work was slow and discouraging. One weekend, A.H. Hulbert was so forlorn that on his return trip to St. Paul he cried out to the Lord, saying "If you won't give me a soul I can't go on." That next weekend Hulbert had his highest attendance at the fledgling First Baptist Church: eleven people, up from their previous high of eight. Two people accepted Christ as Savior that weekend, giving Hulbert the courage and resolve to go on. He and his wife relocated following graduation to plant that church, working tirelessly to see a congregation form and grow. Hulbert would one day even quarry the limestone used in the construction of their first worship center.

Nearly thirty years later, the son of the then-pastor of First Baptist Church delivered a Bible, a gift from the church, to a family down the street. That Bible sat on the shelf, gathering dust in the youngest son's room for three years. But over time that Bible was picked up, dusted off, and read by that young man . . . me. We are all products of the planting of churches, and I am the product of the planting of a church in a small town in northeast Wisconsin. Because someone prioritized that town, I came to faith in Christ. There is a compelling need for the planting of thousands of new churches in thousands of communities just like that.

To sum up, there is a multifaceted Rural Rebound occurring in American society today, and there is the stark reality that lives are changed forever when the gospel is made known. Sure, most Americans will continue to live in urban and suburban environments. Not all small towns and rural areas are idyllic places to live. But millions of people live in these "outposts," and there is an observable trend that suggests that those numbers will continue to grow. It's a trend that tells those of us who are concerned about missions to pay attention. When it comes to spreading the gospel through church planting, smaller towns can't be ignored.

Chapter 2: The Ironic Challenge of the Larger Market

In my experience, church planters ruminate over at least three factors when choosing church planting against established church work as their vocational choice. First, there is the reality that the world is vastly under-churched. There is a pressing need for the planting of thousands and thousands of churches in North America alone. Second, there is the strong evangelistic upside to church planting. New churches are notorious for their evangelistic efficiency. Third, there is an overabundance of qualified ministers available to lead churches that are already established works. From a pragmatic point of view it makes sense for entrepreneurial, catalytic ministers to consider pioneering new works. As most district executive ministers or superintendents will tell you, they are swamped with the resumes of countless "out of work" ministers who are looking for vocational ministry opportunities. Those who can plant a church rather than pastor an established one help to clear space for qualified established church pastors to find a church where they can serve.

With such sound thinking and noble aspirations, it is unfortunate that so few church plants are successful, much less able to survive. Verbal testimony from church planting leaders reveals that only 20 to 40 percent of all new churches planted in North America succeed beyond their fifth birthday. Granted, these are ballpark figures. Many denominations and sending agencies have much higher success rates. In the movement I have been a part of we have seen a success rate of around 85 percent over the last several years. However, as a general rule church planting has a poor success rate.

UNDEREXPERIENCED PLANTERS IN OVERLY DEMANDING ENVIRONMENTS

Planting a new church is a risky endeavor, especially for those engaged in the frontline work of pioneering the new church. Church planters enter into this arena of ministry service usually with great vision as to the future success of the new work. There is great emotional anticipation as they forgo the perceived safety and security of established ministry work in favor of the frontier. They are among the few who follow the Apostle

Paul's conviction of extending the "gospel where Christ was not known, so that I would not be building on someone else's foundation" (Rom. 15:20, NIV). How hard it is, then, for the 60 to 80 percent who never see their churches succeed or survive. Having sought to serve God in a significant way, many ministry individuals and couples who have failed at church planting abandon their calling once their church plant comes to an end.

In my observation, part of the reason that so many church plants fail is that most of the church plants are attempted by underskilled, under-equipped, underexperienced, and undersupported church planters who are placed in overly demanding urban and suburban environments.

TABLE 2: CHURCH PLANT SUCCESS 1993-1997
According to Environment in the Baptist General Conference

District	# of Urban Church Plants success vs.attempts	# of Suburban Church Plants success vs.attempts	# of Small Town/Rural Church Plants success vs.attempts
A	1/2	4/6	0/0
B	0/0	2/7	0/0
C	5/7	8/10	13/14
D	0/3	2/2	0/0
E	0/2	1/1	0/0
F	0/0	0/0	1/2
G	2/2	7/10	1/1
H	0/0	3/5	0/0
I	4/7	6/7	2/2
J	1/3	2/3	0/0
K	4/6	12/14	2/3
L	2/4	6/8	1/1
M	4/6	8/11	0/0
Success Rate	23/43 (53%)	62/84 (74%)	20/23 (87%)

In table 2 the statistical sampling is small, and it is limited to one denomination. Success was defined as a church that had reached a self-governed and self-sustained status financially–or it appeared to be on its way toward self-sufficiency. In my denomination, then, the smaller the targeted community the greater the likelihood of success, in this case 87 percent. The percentages may be skewed on the basis of the small sampling or because of cultural issues. A denomination with agrarian moorings, for instance, may be more adept at planting churches in smaller communities or rural areas, but they may attempt to start new works in urban areas only to find that they are ill-equipped to see that happen.

It may be true that we have, at best, a correlational rather than causational linkage between larger markets and poor success. However, we do at least have a beginning point to postulate what was mentioned earlier: most of the church plants attempted are attempted by underskilled, underequipped, underexperienced, and undersupported church planters who are placed in overly demanding urban and suburban environments. There may be several reasons for this.

To begin, most church planters in North America tend to be young. The ministry of starting new churches may fall into the hands of younger emerging ministers by default because church planting is perceived as being extremely labor-intensive with questionable success rates. Church planting is often avoided by those who could succeed best because of real or perceived difficulties for the minister and his or her family. The planting of new churches falls into the hands of those who have the energy but not the experience and all that comes with it.

Another reason church planting more often falls into the hands of younger, less-experienced ministers is that as the years go by our risk-taking capacity normally wanes. Solomon acknowledged the same by calling upon those who are younger to sell their lives out to their Creator "before the days of trouble come and the years approach when you will say, 'I find no pleasure in them'" (Eccles. 12:1, NIV). Later, referring to increasing fears as the years unfold, he speaks of the days "when men are afraid of heights and of dangers in the streets" (Eccles. 12:5, NIV). The simple reality is that people take fewer and fewer risks as time goes on. Since planting a new church is perceived to carry more risks, experienced people count the costs more readily than those whose whole lives are before them.

Financial challenges and risks make church planting a greater option for the young. Those just graduating from seminary or Bible school aren't accustomed to large checkbook balances, so starting a ministry from scratch is at worst a lateral move financially. Moreover, the likelihood that many of these candidates have young children is less than those who are just a few years older and have already had some ministry success and its resultant financial rewards. Young, childless couples can absorb higher risks. Bivocational work or spousal employment may easily subsidize family income to allow for the ministry to move forward. On the other hand, not many who have years of valuable ministry experience on their resumes will naturally embrace a ministry opportunity if it involves support raising or working bivocationally, which is often (though not always) required by sponsoring agencies and denominations. Many times these ministers have growing families, making bivocational subsistence and/or spousal support difficult or, at worst, virtually impossible.

Many church planters tend to be young and inexperienced. I was twenty-seven when I started a church. Though this does not in any way disqualify them for the planting of new churches, the truth is that other environmental factors will have a great deal to do with the likelihood of ministry success. One such environmental factor is the size and the nature of the target community. I'll say more about this later, but for now I'll make the case that many new church planters end up in the environments which are most hostile to success: urban and suburban communities.

Why do so many church planters, many of whom are young and inexperienced, end up in larger communities? There are several reasons, some of which relate to the sending/sponsoring agency, and some of which relate to the church planters themselves. One reason is that denominations tend to prioritize the urban and suburban locales because the largest unchurched population base resides there. Statistically this is undisputed: where more people live, more unchurched people live. It is reasoned that since more people reside in urban or suburban environments (at least the population density is greater) the potential harvest for the kingdom of God is greater, and therefore we should by all means prioritize the urban environments over the smaller town or rural areas. However, while such reasoning may appear to be sound, denominational leaders often report that much of their urban church planting has resulted in a peppering of small and struggling churches that have never fulfilled their mission objectives.

Another reason that denominations tend to prioritize urban environments (though perhaps not suburban environments) is that there is an increasing awareness and concern that mainstream evangelicals make an intentional outreach effort to minority groups. Certainly this is biblically required. Jesus commanded, "Therefore go and make disciples of all nations, baptizing them in the name of the Father and of the Son and of the Holy Spirit and teaching them to obey everything I have commanded you. And surely I am with you always, to the very end of the age" (Matt. 28:19-20, NIV). The Greek word for "nations" is *ethnos*, referring not to political or geographical alliances but rather to ethnic groups. Jesus forbids any ethnic group from being ethnocentric in its evangelistic endeavors. By the same token, I observe a positive predisposition among Christians in North America to make intentional efforts to impact ethnic groups, who, coincidentally, tend to reside in urban environments. A certain sentimentality may attend such efforts, bringing significant donor dollars to these ventures. Consequently, denominational or sending agency leaders will push for the urban church plant to the exclusion of small town or rural planting. There have been times when under-equipped church planters who could have succeeded elsewhere were mobilized to plant churches cross-culturally in urban environments with poor results.

While sending agencies may lean toward the urban/suburban landscape, the same may be said of many church planters. The advantages of such environments are readily seen: more cultural and shopping opportunities, a perceived higher standard of living, and the simple conveniences of modern living. Others site the same reasons as the denominational leaders: larger population bases equal larger potential impact for the kingdom of God. Planters who grew up in the city or the suburbs are naturally drawn back to their roots, and many who grew up in small towns or rural locations are drawn to the city and the suburbs because they have come to experience those environments during their education years. It is not unusual for potential church planting recruits to say, "I was born in a small town, but I think my real fit is in the city . . . or a suburb." Unfortunately, not all such self-evaluation proves to be helpful in the short term.

Finally, there is the possibility that urban and suburban church planting may be more challenging than smaller town or rural church planting because of stronger spiritual resistance and more varied spiritual warfare realities. As the size of the population increases so too does the sin potential and sin realities of that location. Greater sin may invite significant spiritual strongholds. While small towns are no haven from sin, the argument can be made that as the size of a community increases so too do the incidences of and tolerance toward aberrant behavior. In this regard the spiritual resistance issues become cyclical in nature: demonic strongholds invite the preponderance of sin, and the expansion of sin invites the creation of demonic strongholds. "Which came first?" is not at issue here, but it is possible that urban and suburban church planting can be more difficult than small town and rural church planting in part because spiritual opposition is stronger in the city.

LARGER COMMUNITIES REQUIRE BETTER PASTORS AND MORE RESOURCES

Church planting strategists in recent times have stressed the importance of locating and mobilizing potential church planters only when their suitability for the task is affirmed. Charles Ridley is credited for delineating thirteen behavioral indicators that are helpful predictors for future church planting success. Church planters typically possess:

1. A capacity to realize and cast vision
2. Intrinsic motivation (as self-starters)
3. An ability to create ownership of ministry in others
4. An ability to relate to unchurched people
5. Cooperation of the church-planting spouse

6. Effectiveness in building relationships

7. A commitment to church growth

8. A responsiveness to community needs

9. An ability to utilize the gifts and skills of others

10. Flexibility and adaptability to various circumstances

11. Skills in building the cohesiveness of a group

12. Resilience in the face of setbacks

13. Faith[19]

When such character qualities and skill sets are determined to be in place to a healthy degree, it is statistically verifiable that there is a strong likelihood of success in a church planting venture. Correspondingly, when such qualities and skill sets are determined to be absent or insufficient, there is a strong likelihood of frustration and failure. Ridley, a psychologist, has popularized a method known as a Behavioral Interview, which takes place over the course of a day, to determine if such qualities are resident in potential church planters. Those who possess such qualities are encouraged to continue on their venture; those who do not are encouraged to direct ministry passions elsewhere.

Another mechanism to determine church planting suitability is called the Assessment Center. Success indicators such as emotional health, relationship with God, communication skills, and knowledge of church planting and church growth are explored. The Assessment Center is an event which takes place over the course of several days, when trained assessors observe behaviors and beliefs in a variety of settings: interviews, skill demonstrations, case studies, and group dynamics. Several potential church planting couples are assessed at one time. The result is similar to the Ridley Behavioral Interview: potential planters are told whether it is believed that they should pursue church planting as a ministry aspiration. Once candidates are positively assessed, mobilization to an appropriate target group or environment is the next step.

Mistakes are often made at this phase, because often emerging church planters and movement leaders choose target sites inappropriately and they enter into unrealistic timelines. As one who has directed a church planting movement I can testify that I've made the mistake of allowing properly assessed and qualified church planters to plant churches in environments which did not enhance their likelihood of success. With the deck stacked against them, the price that was paid was enormous. I have seen qualified planters become disillusioned (some of whom even left the ministry). I've seen relationships with church/launch team

[19]Robert E. Logan and Steven L. Ogne, *The Church Planter's Toolkit* (St Charles, Ill.: ChurchSmart Resources, 1991), 2:1.

members become severely injured. And I've observed target communities become "inoculated" against an effective church being planted there for a period of many years. When this happens the sponsoring agency itself suffers with all of the elements that attend failure: strained relationships, donor suspicion, and public relations problems both within and beyond their jurisdiction. Over the years I became troubled as I saw some qualified church planters fail due to environmental factors. By analyzing what had happened I was able to isolate eight important environmental factors which must be considered before deployment. Together these eight factors form a Risk Factor Analysis worksheet, with four factors being weighted with scores of one to five, and four factors being rated one to three.

The four most significant environmental factors we have discovered are:

1) The source and amount of personal funding,

2) The cultural background/affinity of the planter to the area,

3) The number of ministry partners willing to move with the planter, and

4) The number of pre-existing contacts which could possibly play a role as participants in the new plant.

Four other factors which we deemed to be significant though less important than the previous four are:

5) The geographical proximity to a natural (emotional) support group,

6) The actual proximity to the geographical roots of the church planter/spouse,

7) The proximity to other supportive churches, and

8) The level of prior ministry success of the church planter.

On many occasions we have spared qualified church planters much heartache by reengineering the timeline for deployment or by considering alternative target sites by utilizing our Risk Factor Analysis. I am including this worksheet as appendix 1.

Proper assessment and environmental mobilization are essential qualities of any church planting movement. Without assessment based on demonstrable behavioral capabilities and other environmental hazards, the mobilization of church planters is even more risky and haphazard. With that as a backdrop I can now postulate that while potential church planters (even for small towns and rural areas) need to be properly assessed as to their church planting capabilities, some qualified church planters who have failed in urban or suburban environments might have

found success in a smaller community. Why might this assertion be true?
Primarily because larger communities require better pastors.

Larger communities have higher expectations for pastors than smaller
communities do. They have traditionally attracted better pastors for a
number of reasons.

One reason larger communities attract better, more experienced
pastors is money. True, larger churches in larger communities can often
pay their pastors better, but there is more to it than that. Denominational
leaders who play a role in pastoral placement want to do what they can
to preserve healthy relationships with their largest contributing churches.
It is not uncommon for smaller market pastoral needs to be filled by
entry-level personnel, while urban and suburban pastorates are filled by
more experienced and polished ministers. Though denominational executives may be reluctant to admit it, the reality is that their largest revenue-
contributing churches are more likely to be in metropolitan areas. In
order to service these churches and "keep the customer happy," superintendents will do what they can to see that the better ministers go to the
better churches.

Another reason that larger communities attract better pastors is that
larger churches have a greater capacity to attract better ministers. Since
many of these churches are metropolitan, these areas get the lion's share
of qualified pastoral personnel. With larger salaries, staffs, programming,
and greater opportunity for prestige and influence, it only makes sense
that as pastors climb the career ladder the better ones rise to the top and
end up in urban and suburban churches.

The implication is that the bar is raised for pastors who perform in
metropolitan areas. They must be better preachers, administrators, and
strategists than their smaller town colleagues. Conversely, expectation
levels for pastoral performance in smaller communities are lower. This is
not to imply that all pastors in larger communities are polished and that
all small town pastor's are below minimum standards. However, these
generalizations do have some merit. And the implication for the planting
of new churches is that a qualified church planter in a larger population
environment must a have higher minimal skill set than one who plants in
a smaller community. Following this to its conclusion, then, we see that
some qualified church planters who might not succeed in larger communities may, in fact, have wonderful opportunities in smaller towns or rural
areas.

MARKET FORCES VERSUS THE NEW CHURCH PLANT

Urban and suburban communities are competitive by nature. There is
more competition for residents' money, time, and attention than in less

populated environments. There are more options for virtually every service and item available for consumption—more doctors, insurance agents, attorneys, restaurants, and churches. There are more options for leisure activities, more worldviews propagated, and more opportunities for the cultural elite.

When new churches attempt to get started, market realities force pressure in at least four ways: competition with other churches, competition with alternative activities, cultural/political challenges, and the financial cost of doing business. The first of these is the most obvious. Although American urban/suburban environments are far from being overchurched, the probability that some larger, full-service churches exist there is increased. These are the "go-to" churches that have the programming which appeals to established Christians. Such churches do not tend to diminish the numbers of unchurched people in a community, meaning that for the church planter the evangelism market is still wide open. However, such existing full-service churches do tend to diminish the number of mature Christians who could play strategic roles in a new church plant. This becomes apparent during the prenatal launch team development phase of a new church, and it becomes obvious during the succeeding "growth and development" phases when having mature Christians around can be helpful. Most church planters say that they want to start a church to "reach the unchurched," but, as I like to say, they wouldn't mind having some churched people who love Jesus and know how to tithe on their teams as well. Church planters in larger markets must be psychologically prepared to hear again and again that potential launch team members already have a church home with which they're happy.

The second type of pressure that large market church planting faces relates to alternative activities which are available in such communities. This simply means that other non-church-related forces have a significant claim over people's lives, and this force is stronger in larger communities. For instance, other Sunday morning events abound in larger communities. In my home city of Madison, Wis. (population 200,000), my children could play Little League baseball or soccer on Sunday morning as well as engage in a plethora of cultural and educational activities. Fun runs, bike races, fishing tournaments, art shows, and the like proceed without any regard for Christian traditions. The church no longer has an exclusive monopoly for Sunday morning, and this is more apparent in places of greater population.

One related tangent makes the point: the existence of a popular professional sports franchise may make the church's competition with alternative activities even more intense. I can think of two examples. First Baptist Church of Glenarden, Md., a large African-American church in the Washington, D.C. area, pastored by my friend John Jenkins, is only two miles from the home stadium for the Washington Redskins' professional football team. Traffic problems abound on Sunday morning, severely hampering the ability of the church to operate. But First Baptist is an established church with nearly 6,000 members, so the Redskins are more of a nuisance than an obstacle. Contrast that with a church plant in Green Bay, Wis., Oakbrook Church, which met at a high school only one mile south of Lambeau Field, home of the Green Bay Packers, during its first few years of existence. According to Pastor Terry Martell, the challenge of planting a church in a city like Green Bay is twofold: 1) during football season, traffic near the stadium cripples efforts by would-be attendees at Oakbrook to make it to Sunday services, and 2) many parishioners or would-be attendees hold season tickets or obtain tickets to games in other ways, so they are gone to the game. Game-day attendance drops by 40 percent on average. "In Green Bay we hold our breath when the football schedule comes out. Every home game that starts at noon is sure to be a tough one on the church." This is an example of how church planting in larger communities presents unique challenges: competition with the world.

Third, there is the issue of cultural/political pressures: policies related to rentals of public buildings, advertising, signage, and so on are often antichurch in nature in larger communities. On the one hand, planting a church in an urban/suburban environment may go unnoticed by the community at large, which does afford a certain level of freedom for the new church. But on the other hand, many church planters I encounter in such places find that the city fathers, or school boards, or others in policy-making roles have enacted restrictions, for instance, on ongoing rentals with religious groups. There are more hoops to jump through, more forms to fill out, more meetings to endure. The feeling among many church planters is that "political correctness" reigns, and that governmental bureaucracy stands in the way of new churches through the guise of "separation of church and state."

Last of all, there are the financial challenges of doing business. Experience shows that urban and suburban environments exact a higher toll on new church plants than may be found in other, smaller communities. Rental costs for Sunday worship and office space can be challenging. Advertising can be costly without making much of a dent. Eventual land purchases for building permanent facilities can be astronomical, keeping newer churches locked up into rentals for years beyond what might be healthy.

To sum up, challenges to urban and suburban church planting are many, but they are not insurmountable. The Great Commission of Jesus Christ does not call us to ignore difficult situations. However, in some cases church planters with growing (though not developed) skill sets, or those with limited resource bases (financial, talent, and otherwise) will find that the environmental challenges of urban/suburban church planting add enough risk to their ventures to make them fail. It will be shown that these same planters very well may have succeeded in a small town or rural effort.

While the downside to small town/rural living is that there are fewer services and goods available, the upside for the entrepreneur is that there are niches yet to be filled in nearly every market sector. This observation is what gave birth to the business that has become the world's largest retailer and employer: Wal-Mart. Sam Walton, founder and president of the discount retailer chain noted that it was, in part, Wal-Mart's commitment to the small town that propelled them into worldwide prominence.

Chapter 3: What Wal-Mart Knows about Church Planting

Church planting is risky, but it's even riskier in larger communities for the reasons I've mentioned. It probably wouldn't surprise you to hear me say that it's less difficult and less risky in smaller towns, and it's a better option for many church planters. There are a number of reasons.

A BIGGER FISH IN A SMALLER POND

While not backing away from the conviction that church planters should be objectively assessed to assure that they have the skill sets and personality characteristics to qualify them to plant a church, I still assert that church planters for smaller towns or rural areas do not need to be as polished as their urban and suburban counterparts. I know this to be true from personal experience and from personal observation. In my first ministry I was a twenty-seven-year-old church planter assigned to a community of about 12,000 people in southern Wisconsin. Though the venture went well, I can attest to the fact that my skill levels in such fundamental requirements as preaching and administration were subpar. This is not to say that they stayed at that level throughout my tenure, but it is to say that the community offered me an opportunity to grow in my skills in a manner that did not jeopardize the health and growth of my church. Though I may have been subpar by industry standards, I was not subpar by smaller town standards. I have seen this to be the case again and again in the church planting movement I lead. Many who would fail in urban or suburban environments can successfully plant churches in areas of lesser population.

Small town church planters can be less polished than their urban counterparts, and that goes both for skill sets and church planter persona. Preaching, for instance, is a skill set which does not have to be highly acclaimed to be highly valued in a small town. Without being categorical here, chances are good that if a church planter is approved through an objective assessment process this same planter already has some of what it takes to preach decently and thus will be "one of the best preachers in town" in a smaller community. People will "give the kid a chance," and unchurched people, the target group after all, will appreciate a persuasive relational communicator who expresses genuineness in his or her pursuit of God. Preaching does not become the make-or-break proposition that it often is in many other settings. I can think of numerous examples. One planter I coached, for instance, came to his small town as a very weak preacher. We agreed that we would concentrate on the development of this skill. I told him, "When it comes to preaching, either you've got it or you don't. And if you don't, then we'll help you fake it until you do!" He was coached relative to sermon development, energy, voice fluctuation, gestures, and the capacity to move people emotionally. Incremental improvement has been noticed and appreciated by his growing church, and he is now considered above average in his community.

Preaching will often determine which style of church may be planted. Although most church planters will find that a degree of seeker sensitivity will pay great dividends in a smaller town, they will find that they do not need to become radically seeker driven to be known as a contemporary "happening" church in that community. Small town church planters don't need to be great preachers. But the better the preachers become, the greater latitude they will have in choosing a model of church. After all, the stewardship of our lives requires that we work to better our skills for the sake of the kingdom.

Another skill area is administration. While it would be wrong to conclude that small town people are all blue-collar, uneducated hayseed farmers (we have already seen the exact opposite in many instances, related to the Rural Rebound), it is true that relational proficiency will win over administrative adeptness any day in a smaller community. It is important to return phone calls, show up for appointments on time, organize properly, and lead well in any setting. However, in smaller communities the chance that a pastor is viewed as a chief executive officer is diminished.

The same can be said of a church planter's persona. A qualified planter does not need to be able to traffic in the most influential circles of society to be a person of influence in a small town or a rural area. He or she does not have to have the sharpest wit, be the most widely read, or dress from the finest stores to be accepted and respected. The bar is lowered in a less populated community.

All of this is not to advocate for sloppy, subpar church planters in smaller communities. It is not to imply that smaller towns are the perfect places for the refuse of the church planting universe, as if these small communities were the Siberian outposts of the modern world. Competence and an attractive persona will pay appropriate dividends. But the pressure to perform at a certain level is less in a small town in comparison to an urban or suburban setting.

MARKET FORCES VERSUS THE SMALL TOWN CHURCH PLANT

Sam Walton, in his autobiography *Made in America*, makes it clear why Wal-Mart had a fighting chance to become the World's number one retailer and employer: market competition in the discount sector was practically nonexistent in smaller communities. This revelation came about somewhat by accident: Walton's wife, Helen, insisted that they live in a small town.

> "Sam, we've been married two years now and we've moved sixteen times. Now, I'll go with you any place you want so long as you don't ask me to live in a big city. Ten thousand people is enough for me." So any town with a population over 10,000 was off-limits to the Waltons. If you know anything at all about the initial small-town strategy that got Wal-Mart going almost two decades later, you can see that this pretty much set the course for what was to come.[20]

So Wal-Mart began with a small town strategy simply out of family preference; but it didn't take long for Sam Walton to discover that he was sitting on a gold mine. He found that operational expenses were less, and the opportunity to build without competition was incredible. "Actually, during this whole early period, Wal-Mart was too small and insignificant for any of the big boys to notice, and most of the promoters weren't out in our area so we weren't competitive."[21] As an addendum, Walton recalls a moment when they needed to restructure debt to capitalize emerging stores more effectively. When he visited potential lender Prudential, he was armed with his business plan, but the lenders didn't take a small town strategy seriously.

> I had my predictions all spelled out on my yellow legal pad, and I was sure they were going to loan us the money. I went through my five-year plan—my sales, profits, number of stores—and talked about our strategy of going to the small towns where there was no competition and told the loan officer how much business we thought there was out there waiting to be plucked. He didn't buy it at all, told us he didn't think a company like the Prudential could afford to gamble with us. I saved those projections for a long time, and they were all exceeded by 15 to 20 percent in the years to come.[22]

When small town church planting becomes a priority in any denominational or district endeavor where it has been overlooked there will be

---

[20]Sam Walton, *Sam Walton: Made in America* (New York: Bantam Books, 1993), 27.
[21]Ibid., 104.
[22]Ibid., 122.

certain objections from uninformed constituents. However, the payoff for
some church planters and their sponsoring movements, to say nothing for
the advance of the kingdom of God, is notable. The point is that much
progress can be made in such places simply because there are fewer
things for the new church to compete with. It is much easier to fill a
market niche when the market is being completely ignored. Walton,
again, sums up the Wal-Mart "formula."

> Now that we were out of debt, we could really do something with
> our key strategy, which was to put good-sized discount stores into
> little one-horse towns which everybody else was ignoring. In those
> days, Kmart wasn't going to towns below 50,000, and even Gibson's
> wouldn't go to towns much smaller than 10,000 or 12,000. We knew
> our formula was working even in towns smaller than 5,000 people,
> and there were plenty of those towns out there for us to expand
> into. When people want to simplify the Wal-Mart story, that's usually
> how they sum up the secret of our success: "Oh, they went into
> small towns when nobody else would." And a long time ago, when
> we were first being noticed, a lot of folks in the industry wrote us off
> as a bunch of country hicks who had stumbled onto this idea by a
> big accident.[23]

Walton's point is well made, and the parallel to church planting strategies, at least on a macro/regional level, is obvious. Just as major discounters (to their detriment) have historically ignored the small town, so too
have denominations and sending agencies. A reversal of policy is in
order, and many small town church planters have come to understand
this. For instance, Bill Heck, of Journey Community Church in Camas,
Wash. (population 11,000) refers to one advantage to being in a growing
small town. "This community afforded us a great opportunity to identify
ourselves as a church that was very different from the other churches that
had already been located in this community for a number of years."
Early Wal-Mart associate Ferold Arend speaks of the evolution of the
Wal-Mart vision.

> The truth is, we were working with a great idea. It was really easy to
> develop discounting in those small communities before things got
> competitive. There wasn't a lot of competition for us in the early
> days because nobody was discounting in the small communities. So
> when we discounted items it was just an unheard of concept outside
> the large towns. The customers, of course, weren't dumb. They had
> friends and relatives in the cities. And they had visited places where

---

discounters were operating, so when they saw this happening in their town, well, shoot, they just flocked to our stores to take advantage of it.[24]

Discounters and franchises of all sorts no longer ignore small towns, and neither should those responsible for forging church planting strategies. Church planters who may have been swallowed up and ignored in larger communities will, in many cases, find that the smaller market has some advantages. Competition is less fierce, the market is informed and ready, and the opportunities are impressive.

Church growth theorists refer to this as the resistance-receptivity axis, where communities or target groups are ranked according to the natural degree of opposition which may stand as an obstacle to the penetration of the gospel. As this relates to the bell curve shown below, I would postulate that the closer a target community is to being "small town" the easier it is to plant the church. Conversely, the further away we get from "small town," the harder it is to plant the church. I would say that, as a rule, both urban and extreme rural environments are the most difficult places to plant churches.

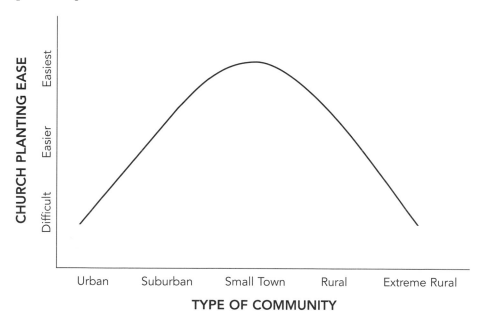

Though the Great Commission calls Christians to extend the gospel to all people groups in every circumstance, Jesus Himself acknowledged the strategic nature of understanding the receptivity of a given market. "Calling the Twelve to him, he sent them out two by two and gave them

authority over evil spirits. These were his instructions: 'Take nothing for
the journey except a staff—no bread, no bag, no money in your belts.
Wear sandals but not an extra tunic. Whenever you enter a house, stay
there until you leave that town. And if any place will not welcome you
or listen to you, shake the dust off your feet when you leave, as a testimony against them" (Mark 6:7-11, NIV). The missionary journeys of the
Apostle Paul demonstrate the same wisdom when he shortened visits in
some locations to prioritize places of greater responsiveness.

> At Iconium Paul and Barnabas went as usual into the Jewish
> synagogue. There they spoke so effectively that a great number of
> Jews and Gentiles believed. But the Jews who refused to believe
> stirred up the Gentiles and poisoned their minds against the
> brothers. So Paul and Barnabas spent considerable time there,
> speaking boldly for the Lord, who confirmed the message of his
> grace by enabling them to do miraculous signs and wonders. The
> people of the city were divided; some sided with the Jews, others
> with the apostles. There was a plot afoot among the Gentiles and
> Jews, together with their leaders, to mistreat them and stone them.
> But they found out about it and fled to the Lycaonian cities of Lystra
> and Derbe and to the surrounding country, where they continued to
> preach the good news. (Acts 14:1-7)

Many times it is wise to redirect ministry aspirations to places of
greater receptivity when bringing the gospel of Jesus Christ. And many
times it is wise to match a person's skill sets and ministry experience with
a location that will receive them. For some, this will mean planting
churches in smaller towns or rural areas, at least in their earlier years, as
opposed to urban or suburban ministry sites.

FRANCHISES AND REGIONAL STRATEGIES

There is something else that we can learn from Wal-Mart, as it relates
to starting more and more new churches. When Sam Walton saw that
his small town strategy was working, the next logical step was to start
franchising the discount stores to other receptive communities. But a
pattern had been observed among other discounters that Walton sought
to avoid: starting stores too far away from the necessary support systems.

> But while the big guys were leapfrogging from large city to large city,
> they became so spread out and so involved in real estate and zoning
> laws and city politics that they left huge pockets of business out
> there for us. . . . We figured we had to build our stores so that our

distribution centers, or warehouses, could take care of them, but also
so those stores could be controlled. . . . Each store had to be within
a day's drive of a distribution center.[25]

The parallel for the church planting universe is that denominations
often make the mistake of starting churches too far away geographically
from other churches and people who can help them. Sam Walton
observed that there was not enough accountability and not enough
helpful support when stores were too spread out. It was Wal-Mart's
desire to capitalize on a strategy of "instant inventory," so that no store
was undersupplied even for a day. For that to happen, distribution
centers needed to be close enough to franchises for a healthy, supportive
relationship. The Bible alludes to the risks involved when isolation
occurs. The people of Laish were completely destroyed when "there was
no one to rescue them because they lived a long way from Sidon and had
no relationship with anyone else" (Judges 18:28, NIV).

Of course, this helped to frame Wal-Mart's plans to reproduce more
and more distribution centers. And from there they began to "stretch and
fill." The idea was to "saturate a market by spreading out, then filling in."[26]
They would start a store about one day's drive from a warehouse, and
then they would start stores in between those two destination points.
And the payoff was significant, not only from control and strategic
support. Advertising dollars were used much more strategically. Word-
of-mouth news about the stores spread rapidly as consumers in the region
interacted with relatives and neighbors.

The parallels to structuring church planting movements are many.
I will deal with these in a later chapter, and in appendix 1, the Risk
Factor Analysis. For now it is worth considering the wisdom of Wal-
Mart. We can build movements by starting new churches in small towns
that are close enough to strategic support personnel. And if we saturate
an area with more and more new churches the payoff can be even
more significant.

---

[25]Ibid., 140-141.
[26]Ibid., 140.

PART 2: PLANTING THE SMALLER MARKET CHURCH

Chapter 4: Understanding Small Towns

UNIQUE QUALITIES OF THE SMALLER MARKET

Society elitists who have spent their entire lives in urban areas have a hard time convincing themselves that smaller communities and rural areas are comprised of anything but backward, blue-collar, uneducated, simpleminded, and culturally deprived people.

> "There's this assumption that when you move to a small town, you're moving out to where all the people have third-grade educations, and all they know how to do is walk behind a mule that pulls a plow," says Dr. Jeffrey L. Tate, a psychiatrist who moved . . . from Houston to Rogers, Arkansas in 1993. "I've not found that to be true at all. People here are bright, educated and well read. They know history, politics. We have stimulating discussions—more than we did in Houston, in part because we have more time."[27]

Sure, stereotypes exist, and there are lots of small towns that fit the stereotype. But the evidence shows that care must be exercised in our presumptions about less populated areas. So what are the general characteristics of smaller communities? John Clayton offers a comprehensive analysis. Small towns are thought to be: safe, friendly, relaxed, gossipy, conformist, boring, remote, married, religious, clean, and quiet.[28]

SAFE

First, they are safe. Smaller communities have lower crime rates. "You don't find skinheads, crack houses, or high rape and homicide rates in Muskogee. . . . *Public Opinion* magazine recently reported that 59 percent of U.S. citizens feel it's risky to go for a walk in their own neigh-

---

[27]Wanda Urbanska and Frank Levering, *Moving to a Small Town* (New York: Fireside, 1996), 17.
[28]Clayton, *Small Town Bound*, 29-68.

borhoods."[29] Violence and crime are not the norm.[30] A friend of mine,
who lives in rural northeast Wisconsin, leaves the keys to his BMW
Roadster sports car in the car so he knows where they are and in case a
friend needs the car. People notice their neighbors and are aware of
unusual activity. Parents do not hover over their children in public
places because there is an assumption of well-being. Small communities
are not idyllic havens, but residents are usually not the victims of crimes.
There is evidence, also, that smaller communities can prolong life
expectancy. "'Living in a large city shortens life expectancy,' states
Norman Shealy, M.D., Ph.D., founder and director of the Shealy Institute
for Comprehensive Care and Pain Management. . . . Cancer incidence is
6 percent higher in urban areas such as Los Angeles and Houston. . . ."[31]
   They may be victims of other safety challenges, however. Because
small town and rural life may involve occupations which are more physi-
cally demanding, such as logging or farming, personal injury from routine
activity may be heightened. When Paul Bland, an African-American
church planter from Milwaukee visited rural churches in northern
Wisconsin on a support-raising tour he was shocked to see a number of
older farmers with fingers or portions of fingers missing. Finally, because
rural areas are given toward greater outdoor recreational activity,
personal injury may be more prevalent. Generally speaking, however,
small towns and rural areas are safe.

FRIENDLY

   Next, they are friendly for at least two reasons: proximity and
longevity. People see one another more often than they would in an
urban environment—at school, recreational activities, clubs, and just in
passing. Anonymity is harder to come by in a smaller town, so knowing
others becomes the rule of the day. The longevity factor refers to the fact
that there is less community turnover in a small, stable community.
People do not come and go as often as is the case in large communities.
Clayton records a poem that appeared in a small town newspaper, which
reflects how small towners view their existence:

   You know you're in a small town

   When you don't use your turn signal because everyone knows where
   you're going,

   When you dial a wrong number and talk 15 minutes anyway,

   When you can't walk for exercise because every car that passes you
   offers you a ride.[32]

[29]Ross and Ross, Country Bound!, 16-17.
[30]Norman Crampton, The 100 Best Small Towns in America (New York: Macmillan, 1995), 433.
[31]Ibid., 18.
[32]Ibid., 35.

The poem is an exaggeration as far as many communities, even smaller ones, are concerned, but the point is well-taken. In the small town people acknowledge strangers, and there is an acceptable "greeting ritual" (such as a verbal quip or a head nod) to salute passersby. Norman Crampton considers this phenomenon:

> Was it Lewis Mumford who said, "Cities are civilization?" If you agree with that idea, as I do, what role do small towns play in civilized life? That's a nagging question to an ex-urbanite, but I think it's answerable. Small towns nurture the essential first part of civilization—civility, the quality of being "adequate in courtesy and politeness, mannerly." This is what small-towners mean when they talk about how people smile, and nod to one another, and motion you to cut ahead in heavy traffic. People don't honk their horns much in small towns.[33]

RELAXED

Small towns are relaxed. The pace of life is slower because things are nearby. Deadlines are not as urgent, sometimes to the frustration of project managers. People dress down, and not many men wear suits to work. Traffic is relaxed because there is little congestion, except for the annual fourth of July parade. People let others cut in line in traffic and at the grocery. "Rural people are a lot more trusting. Roadside stands are sometimes left untended. Money boxes perch on the counters waiting for customers to pay for the produce or flowers they take. It's the honor system at work. People usually don't lock their cars and many leave their houses unlocked at night."[34]

GOSSIPY

Small towns can be gossipy. News of all sort travels quickly, and rumors can abound. Impropriety is known and not quickly forgotten. Celebrity status can be achieved without anything to warrant it. In my own small town upbringing I observed my parents' fascination with the police report in the local newspaper; they wanted to know who was arrested for speeding or any other infraction.

Newcomers can feel as though they live in a fishbowl, but there is some benefit to people knowing your news: "We are interrelated in a small town, whether or not we're related by blood," writes Kathleen Norris, in *Dakota: A Spiritual Biography*. "We know without thinking about it who owns what car. . . . Story is a safety valve for people who

---

[33]Ibid., 3.
[34]Ross and Ross, *Country Bound!*, 27.

live as intimately as that, and I would argue that gossip done well can be a holy thing. It can strengthen communal bonds."[35] News and information travel quickly, both to the benefit and detriment of smaller community inhabitants. Urbanska and Levering take a wry approach to this phenomenon as they caution would-be transplants. "If you have always wanted to be a celebrity, here's your chance! You will be one in a small town—especially when you first move. And unless the town has a large transient element or a significant number of big-city transplants, the fact that you've moved from a big city will qualify you as a person of elevated status."[36]

CONFORMIST

Small towns are conformist: there is a narrower band of acceptable behavior into which people are expected to fall, and the smaller the community the narrower the band of acceptability. Aberrant behavior is just that—aberrant. Conformity is to be expected because of the usual geographical isolation of the smaller community. A smaller population means that friends, neighbors, and coworkers are one and the same. The nature of any group or subgroup is that certain rules of conduct govern individual behavior, so in a small community it is virtually impossible (without strident and intentional isolation) for people to escape wide-ranging conformity. As an example, if the way that business is conducted in a small community is through the local chapter of the Rotary Club, the budding entrepreneur had better join up. In a metropolitan area conformity occurs as well—at work, in the neighborhood, among friends. However, conformity in one venue does not translate to conformity in all other venues, as it does in small towns. "If you live in a ski town, skiers are your coworkers, neighbors and friends, all three. Come the beginning of ski season, you will find it impossible to avoid conversations about skiing. If you don't like to ski, you may indeed find the conformity stifling. The same obviously applies for the central facet of any small town: agriculture, fishing, timber, religion or ethnic heritage. Perhaps what we fear most about small-town conformity is the difficulty of switching brands."[37]

There is one positive aspect to sociological conformity in the small town or rural area: community values are generally reinforced through all strata of the society. The schools will not conflict with the churches, and the churches will not be at odds with the government. Wednesday night is still considered a "no school activity" night in many small communities, a tip of the hat toward the church. If a person's values emulate that of

---

[35]Urbanska and Levering, *Moving to a Small Town*, 20.
[36]Ibid., 27.
[37]Clayton, *Small Town Bound*, 45-46.

the town they will often find the place to be a refuge from the rest of the world.

BORING

Small towns can be, comparatively speaking, boring. The cultural and entertainment opportunities of a larger venue are simply not there, including variety and quality of restaurants, theater, music, art, museums, higher education opportunities, sporting events, and media. This is not to say that smaller communities are bereft of culture. There may well be some quality expressions of theater and the arts, but the variety and frequency of opportunity leaves the culturally attuned person wanting. They seek occasional refuge in a larger community to help fill this void.

Much of the entertainment in small towns is participatory in nature. People not only attend local theatrical productions, but they may try out for a part. And one advantage in the places of less population is that an enormous variety of outdoor activities are usually available nearby.

REMOTE

Small towns can be remote. Because these places are often "away from it all" certain services and opportunities could be hard to find. There may not be a shopping mall, fast food restaurants, an orthodontist, or medical specialists. (However, depending on the community, all of the above may be close at hand.) Fads start in cities and take some time to filter down to the rural areas. One couple I know personally made the classic mistake of taking an early retirement and moving to a rural area where they had vacationed for years—the pristine but incredibly remote Washington Island, Wis. They did have peace and quiet with the other 600 islanders—a far cry from the Chicago suburb they abandoned. But the remoteness was stifling, and within eighteen months they were back home in suburbia.

MARRIED

Most adults in small towns and rural areas are married. People who have grown up there often find a mate through high school, settle down, and raise a family. Common values are assumed without discussion. Because the pool of available spouses is limited, singles often find moving to such a community to be a challenge. Even local singles who have grown up in the area move away, in part, to increase their dating pool and eventually find a mate. A surprising number of these may return one day to raise their family where the quality of life index is high.

When dating relationships and marriages result in a breakup or a divorce, they are more strongly noticed and felt in smaller towns. In a

large community a bitter relationship may dissolve and partners virtually
never see one another again. This is rarely the case in a small town. If a
relationship ends, partners can count on running into their ex-partners
somewhere, and routinely. And many people will know bits and pieces of
their story.

RELIGIOUS

Smaller communities are religious. Church membership or at least
church attendance will likely be a part of the social fabric. Depending on
the area of the country and the size of the community, this fact expresses
itself in a variety of ways. On the one hand, church planting is not
normally viewed suspiciously in and of itself. However, if there is a
respectable church or two in town that dominate the religious landscape
there may be difficulties in acceptability. At least the new church will not
be ignored. It will be "an item" one way or another.

CLEAN AND QUIET

More than their large city counterparts, small towns are generally
clean and quiet. This is not without exception, however. If the community has an industrial-based economy, the location may be subject to a
variety of pollution: air, water, noise and land. Some communities are
defenseless from the greater needs of the society at large, and may end up
host to undesirable enterprises such as toxic waste dumps, mines, or
nuclear power facilities. Much of this depends on the vitality of the
economy. It's possible for litter to be more rampant than in bigger cities:
rather than yards being scattered with fast food wrappers they may be
piled with old automobiles and refrigerators.

The same goes for noise pollution. In most cases a smaller town is
quieter than a larger community. But there are liabilities here as well.
Recreational noise is apparent: snowmobiles, motorboats, and the like.
And because industry may be closer in proximity to the residential side of
town, residents may be subject to other bothersome sounds. I grew up
only one city block away from one of the largest shipbuilding sites on the
Great Lakes. My childhood memories are replete with the noises of the
sanding and hammering of steel, compression tools, cranes, and earsplit-
ting whistles throughout the day and night. When I would return to my
parents' home in subsequent years it was not unusual for me to be fright-
ened out of bed, literally, when the midnight whistle blew at Bay
Shipbuilding. My parents had lived there forever and were impervious to
the sound.

But the popular image of cleanliness still stands. Writes Clayton,
"Despite the myriad of warnings, you can expect a healthier, cleaner

environment in most small towns. Many small-town residents cite air and water quality as some of the most important factors in their decision to live where they do. . . . Many people consider noise a form of pollution, and again, the small town is cleaner than an urban downtown."[38]

While these are general characteristics common to small towns and rural areas, I would be remiss not to acknowledge that each community stands and falls on its own merit. Perhaps the greatest and most helpful factor to consider when analyzing the sociological nuances of any particular town is whether it is a community that is declining, stable, or growing in population.

Communities with declining populations often have lost their economic base; a large employer has relocated or shut down. Younger families are the likeliest to move, leaving the town with a higher median age. Feelings of fatalism may be prevalent. Places with stable populations experience the normal ebb and flow of changing community dynamics, and they are accepting of newcomers and new ventures just as they are accepting of the fact that some people move away and some ventures never succeed. But communities with growing populations may, ironically, be hotbeds of controversy and tension. Something has contributed to the growth: industry, tourism, or national prominence—and not everyone will be happy about it.

> Scenarios similar to those in Santa Fe can be found in Jackson, Aspen, Park City, Sun Valley, and other places throughout the West. As a town is taken over by tourism and more people move in, the population becomes layered and polarized. The old-timers, those who were born there or have lived most of their lives in the area, are most affected by changes as their town achieves success as a resort. They are torn between two realities. They remember former days when mining or ranching thrived, when the population was small and homogeneous and everyone knew his neighbor. Their memories hold pictures of a life that was even and uncomplicated, that moved at a stroll rather than a sprint.[39]

A similar tension existed in Whitewater, Wis., where I planted a church for over six years. Though the highway population sign indicated about 12,000 residents, many of those were college students. The permanent year-round population was somewhere between 5,000 and 6,000. Nevertheless, this town is host to the fifteenth largest business college in the United States. With the population of the university outnumbering the local population, tensions commonly exist between these disparate segments of society. As one professor quipped, "It is as though one day the town woke up to see this large university in its backyard."

When small towns are growing, it is important to consider why, and what the resultant feelings of residents are. Oftentimes the dynamics which brought the growth are changing the entire fabric of the community. The small town may be becoming a suburb in disguise.

> But then the visitors started to stay. Hippies and city folk moved in permanently. Old-timers became resentful because they felt that new lifestyles that they didn't want, need, or respect were being foisted on them. The fancy clothes, French bistros, and health-food markets seemed out of place and supplanted the stores and restaurants they needed, enjoyed, and could afford. Many who lived in these communities all their lives pulled up stakes.[40]

IMPLICATIONS FOR PLANTING THE SMALLER MARKET CHURCH

Having established that smaller towns and rural areas are unique sociologically, let's consider the ramifications for planting the smaller market church. The uniqueness of the smaller market brings with it certain advantages and certain disadvantages.

Because such communities are generally safe, it could be assumed that new ventures, such as the planting of a new church, would be welcomed without suspicion. Such an assumption is wrong. One of the primary underpinnings of a society of safety is familiarity. Because smaller communities are not bastions of change, residents know their community well, and it is this knowledge and familiarity that breeds a sense of communal safety. Thus, new ventures are, at least at first, intrusive. People consider a new church with some combination of curiosity and suspicion. The implication for the church planter is that the process of legitimization becomes essential. Specific steps, addressed in detail later, must be taken to bring the church into society as a bona fide mainstream entity. Church planters should align themselves as soon as possible with other clergy in the area. They should exegete the community, learning its history and political processes. They need to show up at community events, embrace the town as their own, and use the "we" word. Some would argue that this contradicts the admonition of the Apostle Paul to be unconcerned about pleasing men rather than God (Gal. 1:10), but a better understanding of Paul's methodology is found in the defense of his ministry to the church at Corinth.

---

[40]Ibid., 109.

To the Jews I became like a Jew, to win the Jews. To those under the law I became like one under the law (though I myself am not under the law), so as to win those under the law. To those not having the law I became like one not having the law (though I am not free from God's law but am under Christ's law), so as to win those not having the law. To the weak I became weak, to win the weak. I have become all things to all men so that by all possible means I might save some. I do all this for the sake of the gospel, that I may share in its blessings. (1 Cor. 9:20-23, NIV)

Outreach methods may differ from suburban or urban church plants. To begin with, gated or inaccessible communities are essentially unheard of in smaller towns. Door-to-door evangelism or surveying is achievable. Also, because of residents' natural suspicion, advertising efforts which include the endorsement of known local personalities are helpful. The introductory direct mail piece we used in our town included a photograph of a well-known community physician and his wife who were part of our launch team, which made an enormous difference in legitimizing us to the community.

Because small towns are safe, there are certain advantages for the new church. Locating safe sites for services and meetings is easier, since, unlike some urban churches that must supply escorts, people don't fear going to and from services. The same goes for church property, even rental facilities. It is unlikely that extensive caution must be taken to protect against thievery or vandalism.

People are usually open and kind toward newcomers who exhibit a positive attitude toward their new home. The primary implication for the church planter is that friendliness ought to be considered a sacred trust. It is something to be capitalized on, but not to be exploited. And friendliness is not guaranteed. As in any type of community, there may be open hostility toward the new church, its pastor, or its mission. When Anthony and Deborah Perry planted Emmanuel Baptist Church of Thonotosossa, Fla. (population 11,000) they were shocked to be viewed as intruders by some locals. A neighbor to their church property openly declared that he would do everything in his power to shut down an imminent building project. "He stated that all of the families around the church agreed with him. But God led me to speak to another neighbor that I had not met before. He contradicted the angry neighbor and said there was no problem with the church as far as he was concerned." So, friendliness is not guaranteed, even in a small town. But the typically friendly environment means that a proactive church planter will not find it difficult to meet people, make friends, gather information, and gain permission and help from decision makers. A slow and deliberate approach to making friends will pay significant payoffs as the new venture unfolds. People will be open to dinner invitations and social events, and they will not tend to be suspicious of church planters who are genuine, humble, and respectful.

The relaxed nature of the smaller town and rural environment can be a boon for the new church plant. People do have more time than in larger cities, and this can translate into more volunteer hours, hospitality for the church planter, and even time to attend church services. This quality also, in some situations, can mean that church growth and progress will be measured at a different rate than in a larger community. On one hand, this can be unnerving to the goal-directed church planter. In my earlier church planting days I was confronted by a leader in our church who said, "I'm not objecting to the direction of the church, just the pace of it." On the other hand, a relaxed environment means that slower progress will be interpreted by churchgoers without criticism. In many cases, the only person critical when growth is slow is the church planter.

The gossipy nature of the smaller town plays to the advantage and disadvantage of the new church. With word-of-mouth news traveling quickly, it is hard to keep rumor and innuendo in its place, but it is also easier to get the word out about good things when they happen. Lapses of integrity for the church or the pastor are costly. Many new churches have been derailed because the news or implied news of indiscretion (true or not) traveled widely. But good news travels quickly, so when the church is being salt and light, the community will notice. Church planters Art and Lisa Radlicki of Escanaba, Mich. (population 14,000) tell of receiving a phone call from the school liaison officer during the early days of Silver Winds Church. Art braced to hear something controversial, but instead the officer had a compliment. "I was asked if I would meet with a parent of one of the schoolchildren because the pastor of Silver Winds Church was highly recommended in the community for being able to connect with teens and their parents. To this day I do not know who spread that information, but it has produced fantastic connections in the community and an atmosphere of legitimacy concerning our infant church." The lesson is that the small town fishbowl necessitates extreme care in behavior and speech.

That small towns and rural areas are conformist has implications for church planting in two ways. First, it means that the church planter will do well to join groups and attend functions that are deemed honorable by the community. "Are you a joiner? You need to be. In a small town, churches, civic organizations and clubs are the lifeblood of society. If you hate the idea of being a member of a club or organization and detest attending meetings and handling projects, you'd better think twice about moving."[41] Second, it means that the more the church's doctrine and behaviors are out of the mainstream of what is normal in that community, the harder it will be to be accepted and to grow. The first church to allow pentecostal gifts during public worship services, for instance, may have a difficult time getting up and running.

If the typical small town is boring, it means that church life is probably doubly boring. That sad truth means that the church planter with a vision for an innovative church has a wonderful opportunity to fill a market void. And here we are not only speaking of innovation on Sunday morning. New church programming can be creative in every arena: women's groups, youth groups, men's ministries, outreach events, compassion ministries, and so on. Silver Winds Church tried to jump-start a youth program by holding a Hawaiian luau at their facility in the middle of winter. They turned up the thermostat and brought in several hundred pounds of sand. They picked up cardboard carpet rolls from a local flooring company and fashioned them into palm trees. As pastor Art Radlicki says, "We had a huge turnout . . . and then it took weeks to clean up the sand! But every grain was worth it." The new church can take responsibility to liven up a sector of the community that needs to be revived. If the town is boring, the church has a chance to be the most creative thing going.

If the small town is remote, this too gives it a strategic market advantage in the place it serves. By bringing in guest attractions, the new church can serve the community by lessening the remoteness. The church can also help bring the advantages of urban life closer to home by sponsoring events in those locations. Ball games, Christian concerts, adult "nights on the town," and other entertainment options can open new and refreshing vistas to townspeople with myopic vision of the outside world.

The fact that smaller communities value the institution of marriage implies two things. First, programs developed with married people in mind are beneficial. Sermon series, parenting classes, small groups, Valentine banquets, and marriage retreats are well received. Having marriage resources available (books, tapes, videos) augment the ministry. As it is everywhere, small towns are awash in dysfunctional marriages on the brink of breakup. The church planter must be prepared for counseling challenges because, depending on the community, there may be a paucity of trustworthy professional counselors available for referral.

The second implication is that because the institution of marriage is valued, singles will likely feel disenfranchised. This is especially true of those newcomers who have no family or other roots in the area. It is very difficult for singles to move to a small town. A new church which

---

[41]Urbanska and Levering, *Moving to a Small Town*, 26-27.

values marriage but also makes room for singles fills a niche which is often ignored by smaller town churches. Each situation must be tailored to the specific community. Oftentimes it is a mistake to lump all singles together, but it is better to look for ways to assimilate them into the body of the church at large. The town will have its share of divorcees, and something as simple as a divorce-recovery group or workshops for single parents will be considered incredibly novel and helpful.

Speaking of marriage, it is helpful if the church planter is married. Although there certainly must be some, I do not personally know of any modern-day church planters in small towns who did or do so as singles. Moreover, in many places the only religious memory of unchurched people is that of celibate clergy who were out of touch with married life. The best combination for small town and rural church planting is a healthy couple who can model and minister to married people.

The religious nature of smaller towns paves the way for the new church in some helpful ways. The most obvious is that even in a postmodern culture with a fading memory of church life, people in small towns and rural places still respect the church. As long as the new church is postured with legitimacy, it has a good chance of being successful. Most local people, whether they attend a church or not, probably have a faded membership in some church and would identify that church as their church home. Because of this the more sectarian the new church presents itself to be, the more difficult it will be for the church to crack the town veneer. The church should present itself as a refuge for people who have given up on church. This will even be respected by other local clergy if they realize that the new church's target population has nothing to do with those currently attending their church.

The small town church planter can expect to be called upon to perform weddings, baptisms, and funerals for people they have never met. Managed properly, these can lead to wonderful evangelistic opportunities. Because people want a "church" ceremony, often these events take place in the rented buildings of another congregation. The wise church planter publicly thanks the congregation whose building is being used for two reasons: it is appreciated by the renting church and it clarifies to atten-dees that this is not the place to return on Sunday if they want to experi-ence more of the new pastor's ministry.

Chapter 5: Foundations for Planting the New Church

Starting a church in a smaller community does not differ, in principle, from starting any other church. However, there are some particular nuances to be aware of as the art of church planting is applied in this context.

UNIQUE CHARACTERISTICS
OF THE SMALL TOWN CHURCH PLANTER

Let's begin with the church planters themselves. It's true that each church planter needs to be evaluated for potential ministry success through an objective assessment process. Gone are the days when only those who could not find other ministry employment were considered for church planting, and gone are the days when a friendly interview with an eager but ignorant minister qualified for approval. I've already mentioned the two most popular formats used today to evaluate potential church planters, the one-day Behavioral Interview and the three-to four-day Assessment Center. Objective assessment is essential, no matter what type of community is targeted for a church plant. Only those who have what it takes to church plant should do so. Having said that, I now make the case that certain criteria may be held more loosely and certain criteria must be held more stridently for the smaller town or rural planter.

On the Charles Ridley scale of thirteen success indicators, two factors deserve particular attention. First, a "capacity to relate to the unchurched" becomes inversely proportional to the size of the community in which they serve. While it is possible, though not encouraged, for a planter in a metropolitan area to distance himself or herself from the unchurched (maximizing advertising and other draw methods to gather a crowd), it is simply impossible for a smaller market planter not to relate to the unchurched and be successful. One rural church planter describes himself as one who likes to "scratch, spit, and kill things"—referring to his orientation toward hunting and hanging out with the guys. Dick Young, of rural Lingle, Wyo. (population 470) endeared himself to the towns-people and the new church with his willingness to spend time on the ranch, learn horsemanship, and go elk hunting. Ned Reisch of Shadron, Ohio (population 13,000) did everything imaginable to relate to unchurched people, quickly forging relationships with those he met. On one occasion a chance meeting with a private pilot resulted in a plane ride just two days later. Ironically and sadly, Ned and the pilot died when the plane crashed on takeoff. But it was Ned's capacity to relate to the unchurched that left a church of nearly 200 behind only two years after moving to the community.

A second Ridley factor, "responsiveness to the community," also is inversely important in proportion to the size of the community. Church planters in smaller markets necessarily need to embrace and participate in concerns of the local community. Mike Jacobson of Monroe, Wis. (population 9,000) joined the local volunteer fire department before his moving boxes were unpacked. Three years later when, ironically, the Jacobsons' house was destroyed through fire, the outpouring of community compassion and care was powerful, creating a reciprocal relationship between planter, church, and community with lasting impact. Cynthia Schuler of Hartford, Wis. (population 9,400) responded to the local Chamber of Commerce's plea for a volunteer director for a community choir. K.C. Crino of rural Capron, Ill. (population 800) organized a homeschoolers' network and brokered agreements with regional libraries to serve their small town, thereby effectively demonstrating his willingness to serve the community.

Personal integrity is critical for the small town church planter. While all church planters should score well on this scale, my point here is that in a smaller community the biblical admonition to "avoid every appearance of evil" (1 Thess. 5:22, NASB) carries intense ramifications. Any moral or ethical lapse (or suspicion thereof), or even an innocent but poor decision, has the capacity to permanently derail the enterprise. In a larger community, a leadership mistake will result in fallout, but the damage can be overcome because the problem will not become known community-wide, thus not tainting the entire pool of potential church members. In a small town or rural area problems with integrity become known quickly, and they do not go away quickly. As one small town pastor wryly notes, "In a town like ours they love you . . . until they hate you . . . and then they really hate you." Conversely, a track record of solid integrity will become more quickly known in a smaller population environment while it may be virtually unknown in a metropolitan area.

Communication skills ought to be factored into any assessment, but in a smaller community a preacher doesn't need to be great to be considered above average. In truth, growing a church in a smaller community does require some level of communication capacity, but that level is proportional to the size of the population. As I've already noted, many planters with average or slightly below average skills still look good in a smaller town, and with a commitment to growing in this skill they only enhance their effectiveness.

The overarching advantage for the small town church planter is that skills can be developed over time. Tom Clinkscale speaks for many planters as he reflects on his time at Community Bible Church in Charlemont, Mass. (population 1,000). "I was afforded the opportunity to grow in many areas of my spiritual development and leadership abilities. And God grew me into an adept preacher. The expectation for things to happen slowly gave me the chance to plan and implement ministries that could be tweaked over long periods of time."

When it comes to objectively assessing potential church planters for smaller towns and rural areas, some factors matter more and some factors matter less than they do for planters whose destination is a metropolitan area. In general, personal character traits will be more pronounced in a smaller community and personal skill sets, especially if they are learnable skill sets, will be less important. Though small town church planters should not be lax in the development of skill sets, the beauty of the small town is that the lack of competitive market forces means that church planters can grow in their skills over time. This means that some church planters who would not be suitable in a large community can succeed in a smaller one.

INTERCESSION TEAMS AND SPIRITUAL WARFARE

I should have read Ephesians 6:12 when I moved to the small town of Whitewater, Wis. to start church planting, because it would have served me well to consider that the struggle was not one of flesh and blood. I would learn, over time, that even in small towns there are spiritual forces of darkness opposing the expansion of the kingdom of God.

When I first arrived in Whitewater I wondered why there was no middle-of-the road evangelical church that was doing any relevant ministry to reach unbelievers with the gospel. We set up shop in a small office (in a renovated house which had been run-down and subsequently turned into office space) and got to work. I had heard that Whitewater had a storied past, related to the occult. I learned that at the beginning of the 20th century a local resident named Morris Pratt had given himself over to spiritism because he had successfully made large sums of money in an iron ore mine investment on a tip from a spiritist medium. As a result he created the Morris Pratt Institute, which became America's largest school of spiritism. A large, three-story building was built, and within a short time six full-time faculty and up to 45 students at a time were engaged in the training of occultism. Seances and the like took place every Sunday night on the third floor, and old-timers still refer to the building today as "Spook's Temple." The Institute lasted for about twenty years.

That's just the beginning. Our ministry moved forward quite well, and from time to time we would dabble in spiritual warfare. Frank Peretti's spiritual warfare novel *This Present Darkness* was getting popular, and prayer meetings, nights of prayer, and so on were routine. And I, perhaps because I was so afraid of failure, would spend at least two hours each week on my knees in my little office asking for God's help in the work. Five years down the road we had completed construction on our first church building, so two weeks after vacating our office space my secretary and I took the other building tenants out for lunch as a thank-you gesture. Over lunch there was a lengthy discussion about the fact that other building tenants had seen "ghosts" in the office building from time to time. One lady told me that the most dramatic time occurred the previous Halloween night, when one ghost ("a short, Amish-dressed, white-bearded man") was trying to get into my office—but he couldn't. All of this discussion was quite curious to my secretary and me. But it all made sense when it was revealed over lunch that the office building we all had in common—the formerly renovated house—was built around the turn of the century . . . by Morris Pratt. My office was his living room! When we learned this, shivers went down my spine.

This was categorical evidence that Ephesians 6:12 accurately reflects our world. If spiritual dynamics were an important component of the church I planted in a small, seemingly insignificant town, it goes to say that there is spiritual opposition in any neglected community in our world—urban, surburan, small town, and rural.

The idyllic life of smaller communities should not allow smaller venue church to be lulled into assuming immunity from spiritual warfare issues. While it is true that small towns and rural areas are often overlooked for church planting, the evidence shows that part of the reason for that is that the demonic strongholds have had their way in these communities. Apart from the biblical and anecdotal documentation of spiritual warfare, there is a growing secular awareness of paranormal experiences linked to particular places. For example, from 1996 through 1998 at least eight books were published concerning the reported sighting of ghosts and bizarre circumstances in rural and small town regions of my native state of Wisconsin. One author described the flood of responses he received when writing about the paranormal in a rural area.

> After that I was off and running. Calls, postcards, and impromptu visitors brought more ghost stories to my attention. . . . Soon came leads to folktales and more ghost stories. But so did strange calls about UFOs, crop circles, and [the] mutilation of cattle. Within a few

years I had amassed files on odd stories spanning southwest Wisconsin and beyond. The decision to limit this collection to southwest Wisconsin stemmed from a strong sense of place embodied in those stories and the recurrence of some themes different from other areas.[42]

Small town planters must consider it an essential part of their strategy to mobilize intercessors for their ministries. Logan and Ogne, in the *Church Planters' Toolkit*[43], encourage the gathering of at least fifteen people who will commit to routinely pray for the planter(s) and the ministry needs. There should be agreed upon commitments regarding confidentiality, communication, and expectations. Though Christian courtesy may obligate most who are asked to agree to pray, it is important to ask only those who appear to have a genuine track record or passion to seek God in this regard. These intercessors should be contacted regularly, at least monthly, and they should be given an opportunity annually to recommit to the team. Experience shows that there should be one annual commitment time, perhaps at the first of each year, when all intercessors may recommit or decline to recommit. This eliminates the administrative headache of tracking at which point in the calendar year each intercessor joined the team.

The new church, even in its conception or prenatal phases, can exhibit a lifestyle of prayer through a number of means: prayer meetings, nights and half nights of prayer, seasons of fasting, and prayer walks. When youth pastor Tim Erickson led the high school youth group of Bethel Baptist Church of Janesville, Wis. to target the nearby small town of Evansville for a new church plant, they took spiritual warfare seriously.

The youth group organized prayer walks on the first Saturday of each month in their target community while alternating with door to door survey efforts on the third Saturday of each month. The strategy paid off big both for the new church and for the youth group, which developed a sense of dependency on God.

Authors Steve Hawthorne and Graham Kendrick refer to prayer walking as "praying on site with insight." They explain why the physical presence of prayers in a target area enhances the effectiveness of the praying. People see things when they walk which they would miss in their prayer closets. The authors contend that one positive result of prayer walking is locating the "man of peace" (e.g. Luke 10:5-7) in the area—those who would be predisposed toward the expansion of the kingdom of God in that locale. This lessens many of the normal obstructions to the planting of the church.

[42]Dennis Boyer, *Driftless Spirits: Ghosts of Southwest Wisconsin* (Madison, Wis.: Prairie Oak Press, 1996), xi-xii.
[43]Logan and Ogne, *The Church Planter's Toolkit*, 2:6.

Prayer walking opens the way for church planting. Many contemporary church plants begin their efforts with people respected by their community, often using the terminology men of peace. The homes of such people usually draw friends like magnets. Their households become places of easy interaction with people throughout town because of the history of help they have given to their social network.

People who have blessed or helped their communities seem to attract the blessing of God, much like Lydia or Cornelius (both of them hosted the embryonic church in their homes . . .). As you pray blessings of peace upon families, be alert to how God may establish certain households as lighthouses to their town.[44]

Church planting lore is replete with anecdotal evidence that Satan operates intentionally to upset the advance of the kingdom of God. Discussions with pastors/planters in our region have yielded stories of demonic appearances, physical attack, diseases, sleeplessness, and the like. One small town church planter relayed the story of his automobile falling dead on the freeway late one night just as he told his driving companion that his sermon the following day was on "spiritual warfare." Another told of his pet dog's agitation and refusal to enter his study one evening while he worked on his spiritual warfare sermon. Hawthorne and Kendrick quote George Otis of the Sentinel Group:

Spiritual warfare is hard work. It requires us to roll up our sleeves and slog it out. No magic wands. I'm distressed when I hear people talking as if there were some sort of magic wand, as if you could go into one of these areas which for century after century, thousands upon millions of people have used their own free-will choice to welcome demonic powers and principalities to live amongst them and rule over them. Don't tell me we're going to send in a little prayerwalk team to set aside the logical consequences of their free-will choices, pulling up centuries of demonic entrenchment just because we quote a verse or sing a good worship chorus. I'm sorry. It just doesn't work that way. There are no magic wands. But the effectual fervent prayer of righteous men and women avails much. If that verse (James 5:16) were not in Scripture, you and I would be in a bad way today. Fear might have a place in our midst. The next verse makes a point to say that wonder-working Elijah had no magic want at all. He had a 'nature like ours.' He simply prayed 'earnestly.'[45]

---

[44]Steve Hawthorne and Graham Kendrick, Prayerwalking (Lake Mary, Fla.: Creation House, 1993), 83.
[45]Ibid., 134-135.

VISION AND VALUES

It is important that the church planter embark on a process to delineate the values (strongly held beliefs or convictions) to which the church will anchor itself for its guiding principles. Without a strong sense of direction the new church can sail into turbulent waters. Usually five to eight core values will accurately define the church. Values may include such issues as small groups, holistic outreach emphases, relevance in worship, the multiplication of other new churches, the lay mobilization of members according to spiritual giftedness, and leadership development. While some of these values may be preferential in nature (values that the church aspires toward), most should be demonstrable in the lives of the planter and founding members.

It may surprise some urbanites to learn that the values stated for a smaller town or rural church plant could mimic those of an urban or suburban church plant. Just because a population base is smaller does not mean that biblically founded values or the reality of human need is vastly different. Nor does it mean that the values will be more homespun, down-to-earth or uneducated than in a metropolis. The important issue, however, is that when values are articulated and made public they are not offensive, exclusive, or condescending in any way. The new church will become a recognized entity in the smaller town much more quickly than it would if it were in a large community, so image and community goodwill are essential. In an urban environment a planter may get away with a value that states "Unlike many churches, we will strive for relevance in our community and culture," but that would be counterproductive in a smaller town. There is no need seek to impress anyone with creativity or to pit the new church against other existing churches. Better to state such a value simply as "We will strive for relevance in our community and culture."

When values are articulated and appear in written form the church planter has the beginnings of an effective tool to explain, define, persuade, recruit, counsel, and guide the formation of the new church.

The church planter is also responsible to set the vision for the new church: what it will look like, where it is headed, and how it will measure its success. This is where distinctions from typical suburban or urban church plants are noted. To begin with, the ministry focus group is not as precisely defined in a smaller community, with the degree of precision being inversely related to the size of the community. In a large community a good ministry focus group might be college-educated singles in their twenties and thirties. In a small community, such a narrowly defined group would unnecessarily limit market exposure. In a very small community a ministry focus group could be "people without a church home."

The same may be said of demographic studies. While some information may be helpful (such as, for instance, the percentage of college-educated people, percentages of married vs. single adults, or the transient characteristics of the area), a great deal of census and demographic material is of little value. Wise church planters in smaller towns learn more by attending a high school football game than poring over charts and graphs. Personal observations, as well as casual and formal interviews, are of great value. Often the "person of peace" will be the mayor, the local librarian, another minister, or the owner of the downtown diner.

The clarity gleaned from this process helps to guide the style and strategy of the new church. It is not necessary to move the line a great deal in order to become the most relevant or modern-looking church in town. The music does not need to be highly polished to be good. The logo doesn't need to be from a top-level advertising agency to be effective. In general, people in smaller towns view quality with respect, but they view slick professionalism with suspicion.

The name of the church should be progressive but neutral in sound. Church names without the word "church" in them may be viewed with suspicion. Centerville Community Church is better than Centerville Christian Fellowship in many cases. It does not hurt to ask around, seek input from opinion leaders, and draw conclusions slowly. A listing of several possible good names can be submitted to core group scrutiny for prayerful discussion and decision making. If the denomination name does not appear in the church name, then newcomers should be exposed to the denomination in other ways, so as to preserve integrity. Within a week of arrival in our town I was chatting with a local businessman explaining that I was starting a new church. He inquired as to the denomination name, but I was fearful to admit to being a Baptist so early on in our relationship. Finally he said, "Well, your new church sounds interesting, but my wife and I are waiting until that new Baptist church starts. We heard about that from our friends up north."

Over time the new church's style will take on a distinct personality, affecting worship elements, music style, preaching, evangelism, and social issues. The key is to listen, seek input and gain a level of community ownership rather than impose an agenda and style only on the basis of preconceived notions.

WORSHIP STYLES

The worship style of a church is often described along a believer/seeker continuum. Churches which are strongly believer-oriented gear their worship services toward people who are already members of the family of God. They may be more traditional in style, and these churches, though not explicitly hostile toward unchurched people, may have trouble attracting newcomers who are reinvestigating church. At the other end of the spectrum we find seeker-oriented churches. These churches use their public worship services as opportunities to expose seekers, those who are on a spiritual pilgrimage and are willing to investigate the claims of Christianity to Christian truth. Such churches often have an additional service designed for the edification of members who have placed their faith in Christ. This model is often referred to as a "Willow Creek" model, named after the prototype church in South Barrington, Illinois. Finally, somewhere in the middle of the spectrum there are seeker-sensitive churches who orient their worship services toward Christians while being careful not to confuse, baffle, or alienate seekers. One form of a seeker-sensitive church is called the "Saddleback" model, following the lead of Saddleback Community Church in Mission Viejo, Calif.

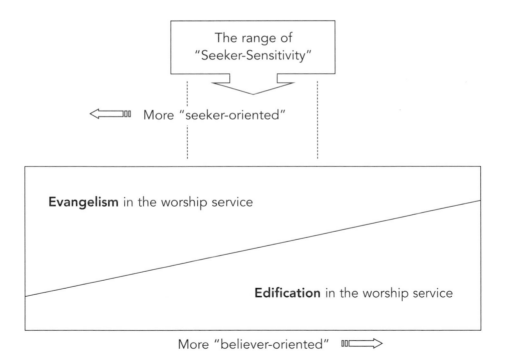

Small town or rural church plants can, in theory, effectively land anywhere on this believer/seeker continuum and do a good job both in evangelism and edification. Two critical issues should guide the choice of a ministry model. First, the church planter must have an adequate understanding of his or her own gift mix and skill capacity. The more seeker-oriented a church is, the greater the skill sets of the church planter must be, especially with regard to communication abilities. Second, the church planter must have an adequate awareness of the talent pool and resource base of the new church. Again, the more seeker-oriented a church is, the greater the talent pool and resource base of the new church must be.

One advantage of small town church planting is that a church planter with undeveloped skills can ease his or her way into a model that requires higher skill sets. In other words, a new church can become more seeker-sensitive or seeker-oriented as the church planter grows in ability. Another advantage is that any level of innovation is amplified in a smaller community; it takes less effort here than in a large community to look new, crisp, and on the cutting edge because chances are that not much innovation is resident in the local churches. A new church does not need to be a Willow Creek model to be the most relevant church in town. In fact, much energy which might go into maintaining the infra-structure of a highly seeker-oriented ministry could better be directed into other aspects of the ministry. Quality should not be sacrificed in pursuit of a ministry model. A church planter who thinks that any drama is better than no drama at all is badly mistaken.

Generally speaking, the larger the community the greater the capacity to be more seeker-sensitive or seeker-oriented. The converse is true as well: the smaller the community the less the line needs to be moved toward the seeker end of the continuum for the church to be known as progressive. Most new churches in small towns or rural areas will do well to adopt a seeker-sensitive model of some sort and commit themselves to doing what they do with high quality. One model which works well and allows a seeker-sensitive church to foray into the seeker-oriented world from time to time is known as the "three-humped camel." Based on the calendar year, most smaller communities have at least three times annually which naturally allow re-entry for seekers: the autumn "back to school" season, the Christmas season, and the Easter to Mother's Day season. During these times new churches are afforded prime opportunity to become more seeker-sensitive or seeker-oriented. A sermon series with accouterments of drama, video presentations, and so forth, accompanied by advertising and word of mouth excitement, can generate increased visitor flow. While these seasons will be more labor-intensive than other times of the year, they allow increased opportunities for outreach despite the fact that the church will not maintain that model for each Sunday of the year.

THE "THREE-HUMPED CAMEL"

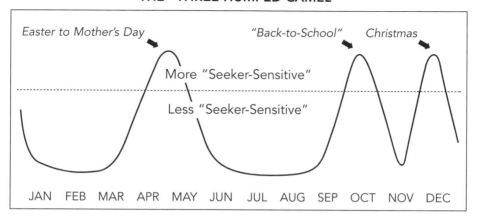

LEGITIMIZATION AND COMMUNITY RELATIONS

The need for legitimization (the process of becoming a known, accepted, and valued segment of a community) increases as the size of a population decreases. There are two reasons for this. First, without a "church" building, the new group is automatically suspect, and murmurings among some people will freely assign the word "cult" to the new church. Second, the smaller a community is the greater the role that peer pressure will play in decision making. The sociology of a smaller community is such that once an entity is taboo, that memory remains intact for a long time to come. Conversely, once an entity is endorsed, it enjoys all the privileges and benefits of full member status. For the purpose of this work we are describing an array of communities, some as large as 15,000 people, so the principles here must be contextualized to specific situations. Nevertheless, it is the job of the smaller community church planter to find inroads into the community so the church being planted is embraced. Jesus said as much when he mobilized an army of disciples to spread the news of the kingdom:

> After this the Lord appointed seventy-two others and sent them two by two ahead of him to every town and place where he was about to go. He told them, "The harvest is plentiful, but the workers are few. Ask the Lord of the harvest, therefore, to send out workers into his harvest field. Go! I am sending you out like lambs among wolves. Do not take a purse or bag or sandals; and do not greet anyone on the road.
> "When you enter a house, first say, 'Peace to this house.' If a man of peace is there, your peace will rest on him; if not, it will return to you. Stay in that house, eating and drinking whatever they

give you, for the worker deserves his wages. Do not move around
from house to house.

"When you enter a town and are welcomed, eat what is set
before you. Heal the sick who are there and tell them, 'The kingdom
of God is near you.' But when you enter a town and are not
welcomed, go into its streets and say, 'Even the dust of your town
that sticks to our feet we wipe off against you. Yet be sure of this:
The kingdom of God is near.' (Luke 10:1-11, NIV)

Jesus made it clear that there is an interplay between target community and message bringer which matters significantly. On the one hand,
receptivity toward the message is the responsibility of the receiver. Jesus
encourages strategic relationships by referring to the "man of peace."
One Bible scholar comments, "If the host has a proper attitude toward
God, he will receive the blessing of the kingdom. 'Man of peace' is literally 'son of peace'–an idiomatic way of expressing not only a person's
character but also the destiny he is worthy of. Such a person would be
open to the kingdom message."[46] The man of peace becomes the initial
host for the itinerant missionaries, providing them an entry way into the
community at large. Similarly, church planters today will find appropriate and receptive points of entry from which to launch an ever-
widening campaign.

On the other hand, the effectiveness of the campaign is contingent
upon the wise decisions of those who deliver the message, who are to
cooperate with community conventionality. Writes biblical scholar
William Hendriksen,

It must be borne in mind that the men who were being sent out on
this mission—at least most of them, we may well assume, were Jews.
But, as has been stated previously, as heralds of Jesus they were
entering Trans-Jordan, a region where many Gentiles lived. That
might create a problem with respect to food. So the Master tells
these seventy-two men to go right ahead and eat whatever is placed
before them, without asking any questions.[47]

The biblical application for those who plant churches today is
apparent. It is critical that church planters be culturally sensitive,
especially in smaller communities where one slipup can be catastrophic.
It is wise for them to build appropriate bridges to people who have the
capacity to influence others in the community. Legitimization comes as
redemptive relationships are built.

[46]Walter Liefeld, *Luke*, vol. 8 of *The Expositor's Bible Commentary*, ed. Frank E. Gaebelein (Grand Rapids: Zondervan, 1984), 937-938.
[47]William Hendriksen, *Luke* (Grand Rapids: Baker, 1978), 575.

The first place to start building relationships is with other established clergy in the community. The level of receptivity may vary from clergy to clergy, but without some level of cooperation legitimization will be an uphill climb. In the small town where I planted a church I almost made a critical error with regard to a direct mail piece. Modeled after something I had seen used in a metropolitan area, the headline was, "At last! A church for those who have found church to be boring. . . ." A wise person in the community, whose advice I had sought, challenged me. He asked, "How do you want other churches around here to relate to you?" In a large community, such a flyer would not be harmful, given the relative anonymity which a metropolitan area affords. But in a small town anonymity is impossible. Thankfully, I didn't follow through. So there are critical mistakes to avoid, but there are positive steps to take as well.

In most cases there is a local ministerial association of some sort, if nothing more than an occasional gathering of clergy. When Mike Evans of New Richmond, Wis. (population 4,500) arrived in town he made it his goal to meet with and pray with each other minister in town, and he vowed to never speak ill of other churches or ministers in town no matter how aberrant their theology might be. The implication for the church planter, of course, is that by joining with the local ministerial association he or she will be cooperating with those on the more liberal end of the theological spectrum. Because separatist fundamentalists by definition will not be part of the group, the new church planter will probably be the most conservative member of the ministerial. In my experience I found myself attending events which were not part of my tradition or agenda, but the payoff was well worth it. Within the first year of my tenure I was awarded the privilege of being the speaker at the community-wide Thanksgiving service, the highlight of the year for the association. It was a wonderful moment of validation for our new church.

Duane Jass of Good News Baptist Church in Mosinee, Wis. (population 3,300) recounts a wonderful story about the importance of relating to local ministers. Shortly after arrival in his target community he met with the other clergy in town. During that meeting he had a heart-to-heart conversation about working together as churches, and he stated his case that all ministers should be open to the fact that some of their parishioners would fit better at other churches. Not surprisingly, that comment did not sit well with the Roman Catholic priest. However, two years later, after making significant progress relationally with all of the Mosinee clergy, Duane was shocked to hear the Catholic priest make a startling announcement at the community-wide Thanksgiving service. He stated, "Our churches all work together, and some in our community who are members at one church might actually fit better at another of our fine community churches." It was a tacit endorsement of the ministry of Good News. Many church planters capitalize on this need to create community goodwill by placing a "church of the week" prayer reminder in their bulletin, sending a signal that they value the other clergy and their ministries in town.

The small town church planter should make it a priority to meet the funeral home directors in their community. In most newer churches there are very few funerals because the median age tends to be younger. What funerals the new church does have from its own membership are often tragic: an automobile accident, a quick striking disease, and so on. However, the reason the church planter should meet with the funeral director is because funeral homes are always looking for spare clergy to officiate at funerals for families who have no church home. Ministers from the other established churches are called upon for this task regularly, but they typically view such requests as an obligation or a nuisance. It will be a welcome relief to the funeral home director to meet a minister who is willing and eager to serve in this capacity. Then, with each funeral the church planter conducts, a widening circle of contacts is made and legitimacy in the community increases.

Relating to government, school, and other institution personnel is critical to strengthening community relations, building credibility, and advancing the new church work. The adage, "It's not what you know, it's who you know," certainly holds true in a smaller town where informal decision making often overrules formal policy. Developing a posture of meeting new people, listening, and getting involved positions the church planter well. One classic story, out of my own experience, involved the need to rent larger facilities for our six-month-old church. Although the year-round resident population is around 5,000 people, Whitewater is host to a branch of the University of Wisconsin. I had developed a good relationship with the dean under whose department all facility rentals were arranged. We had come to agreement to rent a 240-seat auditorium, had drawn closure with our former landlord, and had advertised within the church and to the community at large regarding our move. Then, just a few days before our first meeting at the university auditorium, I was phoned by the dean with some disturbing news. He had been informed by the legal department at the system headquarters in Madison that it was a violation of state statutes for a university to rent to religious groups on an ongoing basis. It appeared that our chances to rent the auditorium were dead. However, within a day the dean returned a call to me. He had spoken to the chancellor of the university about our dilemma, and the chancellor responded, "Go ahead and rent it to them. All the liberals around here are in bed on Sunday morning anyway." So, we had a five-year positive association with the school because relationships allowed for informal decisions to work in our favor.

A final way to build credibility and engender positive relationships is to shop, to the degree that it is possible, locally. When merchants see both the church planter and the new church supporting the local economy they respond favorably. Moreover, while business and price negotiation is acceptable, it is not wise to seek discounts simply because "we're a church." The stereotype that churches do not do the local economy any good and that their tax-exempt status depletes government revenues is only perpetuated when churches and ministers act cheap. As a general rule of thumb the smaller town or rural church planter should "pick up the tab" at every appropriate opportunity. Credibility and legitimization go hand in hand with ministry success. It will be a challenge for the smaller community church planter to gain that status, but the prize, when gained, will be greatly worth the effort.

Chapter 6: **Getting Underway**

With an understanding of what small towns are like, and with a firm grasp of the implications for starting a new church there, it's time to get started.

BUILDING A CORE GROUP

The simple answer to the question, "How do you build a core group in a smaller town or rural area?" is, "Anyway you can." Some traditional methods which work in larger environments work fine in smaller communities, but some do not. However, if done right, there are several strategic advantages to being in a small town which larger communities do not afford.

One traditional method is "farming," a technique adapted from the real estate industry that calls for repetitive visiting of homes, making a casual introduction, followed by letters or return visits to those who seem most receptive. The church planter or team member is not pushy or overbearing. The primary concern is to be relational while keeping an open eye toward the work of the Holy Spirit in people's lives. Follow-up visits can include the gifting of recipients with token items: a refrigerator magnet, balloons for the children, pens, or other advertising specialties.

Many church planters avoid this method because it calls for hard work, dedication, thick skin, patience, and personal vulnerability. However, it works everywhere it is attempted, including in the small town or rural community. I've already mentioned the youth group who laid the foundation for a new church to be planted in a nearby town. Once each month a prayer walk was conducted, and once each month a farming methodology was employed. The strategy paid off quite well; when church planters were finally brought to Evansville a list of receptive and interested people was presented to them to help jump-start their ministry. Plus, the entire methodology got the town talking, laying a foundation for the word to get out. One obvious advantage of farming is that it combines seamlessly with prayer walking to cultivate the field both sociologically and spiritually.

Some keys to effective farming in the smaller community are to be relational, friendly, and nonthreatening. Early evenings and Saturdays work best. The church planter should dress in nice casual attire, not carry a clipboard, be unassuming and ready to talk. "Hi, I'm new in the area, out meeting my neighbors" and other unobtrusive lines can pave the way for a friendly meeting. When receptive or at least friendly people are met, the church planter can ask: "Is there anyone else you can think of that I should meet?" This is a good way to keep an ever expanding circle of contacts alive. After all, especially in a small town, personal referrals go a long way toward legitimizing the new church and its pastor.

Telemarketing is historically a good way to build a core group, but applying it to a small town can be tricky. Popularized in the 1980s, telemarketing was touted as a way to quickly build a team or a church. Even those who dislike telemarketing (it is very labor-intensive and callers must be able to handle rejection) must admit that it works. Otherwise, why would we be continually barraged with those dinnertime solicitations? Will telemarketing work in a small town or rural area? Yes, but at what price?

The problem with telemarketing in a small town or rural area is that the normal anonymity which is experienced in a larger community is absent here. In a large community people would never think to comment to their neighbors that they were called by a telemarketer; in fact, they may never speak to their neighbors at all. In a large community people would never wonder if the person standing next to them in the grocery aisle was the one who called them last week. But in a small town, just the opposite is true. In small communities people talk about everything, including the fact that they received a telemarketing call. And when they see someone new in the grocery aisle, a few whispered conversations reveal that this, in fact, is the new minister who chose to interrupt their placid lives. In my opinion, telemarketing works anywhere, but the price that is paid is not worth the gain that is made in a small town. It's hard to find a small town church planter who endorses this practice. A new church naturally is regarded with suspicion no matter what, and anything that feeds that suspicion is, in the end, counterproductive. It is best to leave this method to those planting churches in larger markets.

Another traditional process for core group development is the networking information meeting. Held as informational desserts or gatherings, potential core group members are invited to learn about the new church, its purpose, vision, values, and timeline. This works well in small town or rural environments because, again, relationships mean everything. It is especially helpful to have a new church prospectus available for participants. The prospectus can come in the form of a spiral bound notebook which articulates the characteristics of the new church. In addition to the vision, values, methods, and timeline information, the prospectus should include letters of recommendation that endorse the church planter to the new community. Such letters can come from virtually anyone who has had a personal or professional relationship with the planter: ministers, bankers, school teachers, employers, and so on. These will go a long way toward establishing credibility in the community. Depending on the situation, networking meetings can be held in a private location, such as a home, or in a public location such as a community center or school.

Networking, incidentally, begins at day one and appears in various forms. Bob and Cynthia Schuler of Hartford, Wis. (population 9,400) held a well-attended open house when their new home was built. It served as a launching pad for a neighborhood Bible study. Some suggest having a garage sale after arrival in the new town, rather than prior to leaving the former location, as a way to make new contacts. Community involvement of any kind usually has a high payoff in a smaller town. In the community that I church planted I played more softball games in the co-ed league than I cared to. I hate playing softball. It is on my "never need to do it the rest of my life" list. But playing on a softball team, and eventually having a church team that played in the city league, became an enormous base for contacts and legitimization. Mike Sechler, of Spearfish, S. Dak. (population 8,000) joined an early morning basketball league at a local gym. In the process he met a Christian man who became a key source of information about Spearfish. Two months later the man told Mike, "My wife and I really believe God is calling us to your church plant. Can we talk?" They became key people in the core group—and they brought four other families along as well.

Advertising to build a core group works well in smaller communities, as long as the advertising is presented in such a way so as not to cause a rift between the new church and other churches in the community. This is where the small town has such an advantage over the larger community. To begin with, few, if any churches in smaller towns advertise, giving a new church a strategic advantage. (Once the new church establishes itself in the smaller town, it can be expected that other established churches will also begin to advertise in response to market pressures.) Second, costs are minimal for virtually every media: newspaper, direct mail, radio, or cable television, and many avenues for free advertising are available. Third, advertising gets much more notice in a smaller community than it does in a metropolitan area. Mike Sechler (Spearfish, S.Dak.) placed an ad in the "help wanted" section of the local newspaper that said, "New church starting, needs your help."

Consider the small town newspaper; several factors favor those who plant churches. Often these newspapers come out once or twice a week, so people read everything in them. They read letters to the editor, school board news, high school sports, the generous check which the Rotary Club is giving to the retirement home, and who got arrested for speeding.

And they pay attention to the new church in town. Nearly everyone in town subscribes to the paper, so the readership is significant. And small town newspapers are always looking for copy. Rather than waiting for the local reporter to show up and do a feature article about the new church, the small town church planter can create his or her own story and submit it along with a complimentary photo. It will appear the following week, perhaps on the front cover. Russ Shearer of Algoma, Wis. (population 3,500) describes the instant notoriety he and Tina received when their story appeared in the *Algoma Record Herald*. They were immediately recognized around town, helping to legitimize their effort. One other way to capitalize on the small town newspaper is to utilize the Letters to the Editor section. This section is often the reposi-tory of the town scuttlebutt; anyone who has a gripe, a compliment, or an issue to raise will submit a letter to the editor. And everyone who receives the newspaper will read those letters. The church planter who occasionally sends a complimentary note to the "warm, receptive, and neighborly folks of our fine community" will not only engender goodwill, but he or she will continue to remain visible to the community at large. Also, especially when building a core group, classified ads can get the word out. They are inexpensive and widely read.

A concluding point regarding the newspaper: While it is true that the church planter can expect some free publicity, the surest way to develop that publicity flow is to be a business partner of the newspaper. From the perspective of the planter, the advertising is cheap, but to the small town newspaper manager the investment the new church makes is greatly appreciated. The newspaper owner will be surprised to meet a minister who is not always looking for free press and actually wants to pay for services rendered. The money spent as a regular customer will more than pay for itself in other ways. I well remember a time when our new church hosted a special dessert outreach with a prominent member of the Green Bay Packers football team as our special guest. We paid about $50 for an eighth-page advertisement in the *Whitewater Register*, which included a photograph of the football player. On the following page, in the sports section, an article appeared about the upcoming event, with a photograph twice the size as the one we had paid for.

Direct mail works well in small towns and rural areas. It is inexpen-sive and easy to do. It is not necessary to contract with a big-name marketer to make direct mail work well; in fact, it may be better to have something made closer to home with a professional but not flashy look. Having local businesses contributing to the outreach effort is preferable to having something slick show up unexpectedly in the mailbox. It is good to become acquainted and friendly with the postmaster, because the local post office can be an ally rather than an obstacle to the direct mail plans.

In many smaller towns the post office will arrange a specific date for mail delivery as opposed to a "guestimate" in a larger community. Before spending considerable sums on mailing labels from a national service, church planters in small towns should consult local sources. Often the electric utility will print labels from its customer base very inexpensively and with up-to-the-minute accuracy. The post office may also allow the church planter to sort rural carrier routes with no labels at all, saving considerable time and expense.

Other forms of advertising are worth noting, and they can serve the new church both in the developmental core group phase and in succeeding growth phases. Church planters who have an office in the community, rather than in the home, gain instant recognition and legitimacy. The sign on the window makes a big difference to passersby. The sign should clarify that this is the church office, not where the church meets for weekend services. Townspeople do not need the impression that the entire church can meet in a little office. An ad in the telephone Yellow Pages is a priority. It's doubtful that any other churches are placing display ads, so the new church can attain instant credibility and visibility with a small investment. Community-access cable television may provide another outlet for getting the word out, as will local radio. The downside with small town radio stations, however, is that their market segment typically (not always) caters to older adults who would be less likely to have interest in a new church. The new church should also have an Internet web site. Smaller communities are not necessarily "hick towns;" educated and Internet-savvy people are everywhere. Another simple method of advertising in the smaller town or rural area is the printed flyer, which can be stapled or thumbtacked all around town. Tear-off flyers with the telephone number and other information can easily be produced with desktop publishing programs and placed in laundromats, convenience stores, bank lobbies—just about everywhere. And when specific events are advertised (such as the launch or grand opening of the church) local proprietors often allow the new church to place the flyer in the front window of the shop. This type of activity builds relationships and offers opportunity for helpful and redemptive conversations. Follow-up interaction occurs, of course, following the event when the church planter or team members sweep through town to take down the flyers which were posted the week before.

Community involvement of any type becomes, essentially, advertisement. One launch team (core group) member of a small town church plant came up with a great way to capitalize on the town's annual Fourth of July parade. As a Volkswagen automobile salesman, he had access to a newly released 1990s version of the Volkswagen Beetle. The car was then decorated with signage that mentioned the new church along with the phrase "Just Putting a Little Bug in Your Ear." The cute and easy strategy paid off well, with many telephone inquiries made during the following week. Another church began a tradition each summer with a "Cancel the Summer Slump" weekend, when church members were asked well in advance to plan to not be on vacation. The culmination was a big picnic at the park—with a special surprise, to be revealed at the picnic. One year the special surprise was a camel. Later it was a circus elephant, and so on. These events would be ignored in a metropolitan area, but not in a small town. The event caught on so well that it is covered each year by local media.

A proven method to build a core group that works well in smaller communities is the Sneak Preview Service, which gives the church planter the opportunity to showcase the new church to potential core group members prior to the time when it is fully operational. The idea behind a Sneak Preview Service is that from time to time (perhaps every six weeks at the beginning) the church is able to have a full-fledged worship or seeker service that demonstrates what the church will look like on a routine basis once it is launched. The event does not neces-sarily need to be held on a Sunday morning. It can be well-advertised as an event to "come check us out." David Howie, church planter in Lake Geneva, Wis. (population 9,000) massively advertised the first preview service of Lakeland Community Church through direct mail, and held the service on a Sunday evening. Several hundred attended, and the event served two purposes: 1) it helped to recruit potential launch team members and 2) it helped to inform the community at large of the legiti-macy and style of the church.

Sneak Previews can be especially helpful in a smaller town or rural area because they help accelerate the legitimacy of the new church. More so than in a larger town, the church is held in suspicion by the commu-nity at large until it has Sunday morning services. If there is general knowledge that a new religious entity is in its formative stage, but the group is meeting in a home or in some small community room, there is greater likelihood that the church or group will not be considered mainstream. A Sneak Preview gives the church a chance to showcase itself and inform others that the church is on its way . . . though not quite ready to have services each week. For more on Sneak Preview Services see appendix 2.

LAUNCHING THE NEW CHURCH

As the core group (launch team) matures, eventually the church will meet its objective of launching to public status, when it operates as a fully functional and recognized church. While most standards and procedures for the launching of the smaller community church parallel those of any new church in any size community, some allowance is made with regard to the contextual issues of the smaller town.

In the movement I have led, for instance, we seek to have at least forty active adults committed to a launch team prior to the public opening of the new church. The standard has been established with the rationale that this number of active participants is necessary for infrastructure to be adequate to handle the new church once it is up and running. We have observed that generally speaking a new church will be two to three times the size of its core group one year after it has begun public services. There will be personnel needs for Christian education, worship services, small group leadership, hospitality, and so on. In truth, this standard is laudable, and even achievable, for many smaller communities. Premature launches are listed by Steve Ogne and me as one of the top issues in the coaching of successful new church planters. When churches start with an inadequate infrastructure a severe price is paid in terms of the ability to maintain and build the new church. As with premature human beings, some issues which hamper the new church prior to its public birth will remain evident well into its life span.

Launch team size standards should be achieved whenever possible in a smaller community. However, there is a unique interplay between the size of team and the gestation period which must be monitored in small towns or rural areas. Church planters must be wary of the prodding of launch team members to launch soon because "lots of people out there say they're going to come as soon as we start regular services." Steve Ogne calls this the "if we launch it they will come" syndrome, advocating that church planters press for being health-driven rather than calendar-driven.[48] But there are two issues which may make allowance for smaller launch team sizes in the smaller town. One is that, depending on the size of the community, it may simply be unrealistic to find forty enthusiastic adults prior to launch. In some rural areas or isolated communities the population base may be so small as to warrant public services with a skeleton core group. In these cases a church planter can seek temporary help from other regional churches which may have an interest in seeing the new church start successfully. These "short-term missionaries" can sign on for a period of six to twelve months to play a strategic role in the operation of the church. However, it still may be unrealistic to produce a launch team of forty members.

A second reason to make allowance for launch team size in a smaller community is that, as stated earlier, the launch team will not enjoy the anonymity they would in a large community. In the small town the

[48]Steven L. Ogne and Thomas P. Nebel, *Empowering Leaders through Coaching* (St. Charles, Ill.: ChurchSmart Resources, 1995), 7:6.

launch team is a known entity, and the longer they meet in homes without having a public worship routine, the more they risk being seen as illegitimate in the community. If the new church were starting in a metropolitan area and it decided to delay the launch for another six months to grow the infrastructure, no one would notice and no one would care. However, in the small town the community "grapevine" may, in some cases, require that the entity go public prior to its ideal size. The price to pay for delaying may not be worth the gain in growing the launch team substantially. In fact, the delay may pollute the church planter's efforts to recruit more launch team members because genuine prospects may become suspicious of the group's secret status.

LOCATION, LOCATION, LOCATION

One critical milestone toward the launch of the new church will be acquiring space for worship facilities. Obviously, options decrease as the population decreases. Often the best opportunity will be to rent a local school, if possible. Many times the rental of a school in a small community does not entail the endless red tape of a large community. Danny King, a key layperson at New Hope Evangelical Free Church in Cedaredge, Colo., says that renting the local high school worked well in the early days. "The rent was very reasonable. The principal was invited to attend our services, and he's done so several times. One of our members was a teacher there and helped considerably with the liaison." Church planters Bill and Shirley Heck cite the ability to work well with a school as factoring into their decision to plant Journey Community Church in Camas, Wash., rather than in a larger community. "Though they were resistant at first, they were open to having us use the new middle school—an ideal location for us that represented the kind of values and approach to ministry that was uniquely ours."

It should be noted that school auditoriums often require less setup than many other locations, so there will not be a necessary cash outlay to purchase seating. An increase of rental revenue is often appreciated by the school administration. Since the building is a community focal point, instant legitimization will come should the church meet there. One liability, however, is that schools are notorious for not having storage space—or at least not making it available. However, this is not always the case. I have found that school rentals in small towns are generally inexpensive, and I recommend that church planters offer to pay more than they are being asked to pay. The gesture will result in goodwill—and it will be remembered when favors are needed.

A solid relationship with a local realtor will bring many leads. Storefronts, VFW halls, movie theaters, community centers, and daycare facilities have all been used in smaller communities to start new churches. One advantage in the smaller town is that rentals are usually affordable. In many cases it is to the advantage of the church planter to offer a little more than the landlord requests. This small gesture fosters goodwill all around and will rebound in reciprocal favors. There may also be opportunity to rent a facility which is available seven days per week, rather than just for Sunday worship.

The important issue to keep in mind with rentals is legitimization or image. If another new church, perhaps several years ago, attempted but failed to get started in a given location, the church planter must be wary about residual image issues. In one small town several fledgling groups tried to start but failed at the old YMCA building. Finally a church planter came along who started a church in a hotel conference room to distance this church from the obvious choice. Smaller communities have longer memories. Whatever location is settled on, it should be, to the degree possible, a place which reflects the new church as an organization with a future, rather than as a "fly by night" group.

WHEN TO LAUNCH

Determining the time of the year to launch depends on regional and local factors. Summer launches are rare in urban settings and almost unheard of in smaller communities for the obvious reason that most small town inhabitants utilize summer as a vacation and getaway season. Spring launches, closer to Easter, have some merit. However, there are three mitigating factors to consider with an Easter-oriented launch. The first is that daylight saving time often begins around Easter, which gambles the possibility that some newcomers, already risking by venturing out to the brand new church, will confuse the time of the service and forever miss attending the church. The second factor is that many school districts coordinate their spring breaks with Easter, meaning that many families will be out of town on the weekend, or even for two weekends if they're gone for a week. Unlike many larger communities, small town public and parochial school calendars usually coordinate across the board: the high school spring break is the same as the elementary school spring break, and so on. The third factor is that Easter is followed by summer and the summer slump. The liability here is that by the end of summer, just prior to the fall growth season, most of the history of the new church has been during the summer slump. This can exact a psychological toll on both the church planter and the launch team, thus hampering the potential growth of the new church. During our first summer I didn't exactly display great leadership and maturity when I looked out one Sunday at the thirty-three attendees and opened the service with, "Where is everybody?"

Winter is a good launch time for smaller communities and rural areas, especially in northern regions when recreational opportunities are fewer due to weather factors. The birth of the new church just prior to Christmas can capitalize on the season by advertising a special Christmas series in conjunction with the new church. This brings automatic legitimacy to the new church. Most residents figure that if the church celebrates Christmas it must be in the mainstream. One downside is that the time between Christmas and New Year's Day often means furious family travel, again depleting the potential attendee pool.

Most church planting strategists still consider the fall season, after Labor Day and at the beginning of the school calendar, to be the best time to launch a new church. That is true in small towns and rural areas as well, when life again becomes routine. A successful fall launch carries with it the advantage of capitalizing on the renewed predictability of life, but it also allows for an entire ministry year to occur prior to the summer slump. This allows infrastructure to mature and for growth momentum to be maximized.

I offer two final thoughts regarding the time of the year when the new church launches. First, the wise church planter will not rely strictly on hunches and intuition to make the launch decision but will seek out the local pulse of the community. For instance, in many areas of the upper Midwest, September is considered the last month of summer. People still venture away for weekend trips to the cottage or to enjoy the autumn colors. In some places, October will fare much better than September for a launch effort, but be aware of the Sunday when daylight saving time changes back to standard time. Second, it is helpful not to use the terms "launch" and "grand opening" synonymously. New churches in smaller markets should habitually capitalize on any momentum-making opportunities. By delaying the use of "grand opening" until a later time (perhaps six months to a year), the new church can, in essence, launch twice. During the interim, church systems are becoming more mature, and the church planter can "buy time," so to speak, with the new congregation by casting vision for the future without needing to apologize that the new church is not a full-service church quite yet. This parallels the thinking of Rick Warren, whose "purpose-driven" church model takes advantage of crowd-gathering strategies with intentional assimilation programs.

> Once you've gathered a crowd of attenders you must begin the important task of forming them into a congregation of members. The crowd must become a church. . . . Assimilation is the task of moving people from an awareness of your church to attendance at

your church to active membership in your church. The community talks about "that church," the crowd talks about "this church," but the congregation talks about "our church." Members have a sense of ownership. They are contributors, not just consumers.[49]

By capitalizing on momentum events followed by seasons of assimilation a newer church in a smaller market can keep reaching out without waiting for all ministry systems to be operational and mature.

PRAYER AND SPIRITUAL DYNAMICS

Although an intentional spiritual dynamic accompanies the new church from its conception, it becomes especially important that reliance on God be evident leading up to and through the launch phase. As was established earlier, small towns and rural areas are not exempt from the grip of evil; in fact, the dearth of Christian witness may be due, in part, to spiritual strongholds. When Ed Rafferty moved to plant Cedar Creek Community Church in Grafton, Wis. (population 9,000) he personally prayerwalked around the circumference of the community several times, carrying this habit through to the launch season as well. (A beneficial byproduct, according to Ed, was that this habit helped him to lose weight and stay in shape.) When Faith Community Church of Hudson, Wis. planted a daughter church in nearby New Richmond, hundreds of people showed up for a community-wide prayer walk, leading to a successful launch. David and Phyllis Howie knew that when they launched Lakeland Community Church in Lake Geneva, Wis. (home of the occultic Dungeons and Dragons fantasy role-play game) there would be spiritual opposition to their efforts. They enlisted the help of a group of intercessors from their home church in Atlanta, Ga. to come during the launch weekend to prayer walk and intercede on behalf of the work. Other church planters have called on their launch teams to special prayer events, times of fasting, or consecration. Prayer calendars and e-mail can keep intercessors on track and well-informed as the project unfolds.

ADVERTISING

Just as advertising is an important method of launch team building in the smaller town or rural area, it is an essential tool for the launch and beyond. Again, the advantage in smaller communities is that so many affordable advertising options are available for the new church. Direct mail will usually give the best payoff. A piece that advertises an ongoing sermon series (perhaps for six to eight weeks—with catchy sermon titles included) has a longer shelf life than a simple announcement piece.

[49]Rick Warren, *The Purpose-Driven Church* (Grand Rapids: Zondervan, 1995), 309.

A nicely done direct mail piece by a church will find its way on to the refrigerators of many small-town residents. Ideas can be garnered from other church planters or from professional layout agencies. Brian and Cherie Rudesill of Hidden Valley Community Church in Dodgeville, Wis. arranged to have a series of three direct mail pieces delivered to their area for the three weeks leading up to their launch. Some townspeople will resent receiving direct mail from anything religious and will find a way to express their displeasure, but this is normal and inevitable.

One alternative to direct mail in the smaller community is to include the piece as an insert in the local newspaper or shopper-advertiser. Art and Lisa Radlicki (Escanaba, Mich.) creatively work the classified sections of such papers. "We find a category like Household, To Give-Away, Sportsman, etc., and we will put something in there. Once, in the Household section we mentioned that attending our church was beneficial for the entire family. We actually have a group in our church that calls themselves 'Section 67,' that comes up with creative ways to advertise there." And the costs are easy to absorb: four weeks, 15,000 homes, $20.

Some level of newspaper advertising is warranted at launch time, primarily to inform and to legitimize the birth of the new church. However, a self-written article presented to the editor with accompanying photographs leading up to the event will truly make a difference. Also, the editor should be invited to attend and report on the first service. In most cases he or she will be glad to do so.

Church planters should not ignore other cost-effective methods of advertising. Simple desktop published flyers can be placed virtually everywhere around town. Door hangers work, too. Launch team members can be given personal invitations to mail out, perhaps at a launch team addressing party. A personal letter can go out to everyone the church planter has met so far, even if they already have a church home. The text of the letter can be respectful of that possibility, asking that if they do have a church home that they consider coming along one Sunday as an encouragement to the planter—or asking that they pass along the news to someone who may be searching for a church home.

Any materials that go out to the community must be scrutinized and re-scrutinized by reliable people, since oversights (such as forgetting to place a telephone number or time for the service) are common for inexperienced advertisers. Advertising should be professional, but it does not need to be slick to attract attention. In a small town every effort should be made to advertise in every way possible. The objective is not to overwhelm the community, but to encourage and inform effectively.

Because this is a small town or rural church plant a certain protocol is in order when the church goes public. Inclusive language must be used both verbally and in written form. "We're glad to be, along with the other fine churches of our area, a part of the spiritual heritage of our community" is better than, "Finally, a relevant church has come to this needy town." Some small town church planters specifically mention another church from the community each week during their worship services, and refer to that church in the bulletin as the "Church of the Week" to pray for. If it is possible to get a letter of welcome from a local politician, such as the mayor, to read at the first service, it will also build the legitimacy of the new church. Another bit of protocol is to remember that the smaller the town is the greater the likelihood that attendees will recognize if someone else is not a local resident and consequently be suspicious of an unfamiliar crowd. Well-wishers from parent churches or from the church planter's home will certainly want to catch the excitement of the new church, but they should be encouraged to stagger their visits, phasing them in over the course of the first month so that not all show up at once. It is not helpful to the growth and self-image of the new plant to have an enormous crowd on its launch Sunday followed by what are perceived to be meager attendance levels.

Launching a new church in a smaller community is an exciting and noticed event. Wise church planters proceed incrementally and with patience, recognizing that God is about the business of building His church in His timing.

Chapter 7: Post-Launch Momentum and Growth

Rarely do new churches start as well as church planters anticipate they will. It is axiomatic that church planting is harder than the church planter thinks it will be, even when the church planter knows it will be challenging. Much of the psychological and actual energy expended before the launch is on getting the church public, "doing church." Once the new small town or rural church has launched, the venture is susceptible to what Steve Ogne and I refer to as "Post-Launch Syndrome."[50] Though the church planter anticipated steady and perpetual growth, he or she now comes face to face with the fact that such growth does not come without intentionality. And the equation has changed: a great deal of energy is consumed by creating every Sunday service and keeping the machinery running. Two areas which suffer the most following the birth of the new church are leadership development and evangelism/outreach.

LEADERSHIP DEVELOPMENT

Leadership development becomes critical because the growing church needs the infrastructure and delegation mechanisms to allow for expanded ministry. There are mechanisms such as leadership communities, which occasionally gather for inspiration, troubleshooting, and vision casting, which can be of considerable help to the church planter. Carl George's meta-church model endorses the Vision-Huddle-Skills format for occasional leadership gatherings.[51] The helpful format can keep leaders growing, inspired, and connected without burdening them with excessive meetings. It is easily adapted to smaller town or rural contexts.

Choosing a leadership board is critical, especially in a small town. This issue is amplified in a smaller community because whenever friction or misunderstandings occur there can be significant repercussions. News travels more quickly and thoroughly than in a large community.

When official church boards are poorly chosen, more grief comes into the lives of both the church planter and potential leaders than perhaps any other issue in the early months of the church plant. Time and again smaller town church planters are wearied by complications within their leadership teams, and I have seen well-meaning lay leaders sacrifice time

---

[50]Ogne and Nebel, *Empowering Leaders Through Coaching*, 7:7.
[51]Carl F. George, *Prepare Your Church for the Future* (Grand Rapids: Revell, 1991), 135-148.

and effort, only to become frustrated and disillusioned with church life. Curiously, the New Testament warns planters/pastors to be careful in choosing elders ("Do not be hasty in the laying on of hands. . . ." 1 Tim. 5:22, NIV), but it also warns potential lay leaders to be careful in accepting leadership positions ("Not many of you should presume to be teachers. . . ." James 3:1, NIV).

The basic difficulty is disharmony over value and agenda. In other words, as time goes on the leadership team discovers that they are at odds with one another (sometimes with the pastor) over certain issues affecting the direction of the church. This is not unlike a marriage, where partners discover that they "thought they knew" what the other person was like, but then find a completely different picture.

But unlike marriage, where the partners work things through because of their pledge to stick together "for better or worse," leadership teams in new churches operate on an entirely different set of assumptions. When care has not been exercised in choosing an initial leadership team and wrong assumptions have been made relative to the purpose and tenure of that initial leadership team, the result is painful for everyone.

There are several reasons such difficulties occur. First, there may have been leaders on site prior to the arrival of the church planter. These leaders had the initial vision for the new church, and they had already been making decisions about the new church. It is natural (though not necessarily healthy) for them to assume that they will be the future leaders of the church. The church planter must come according to their terms. When it is discovered that differences exist among leaders tensions mount.

A second reason this disharmony may occur is that the church planter is often insecure. Church planters are often new to pastoral ministry, or at least new to the role of being the senior pastor. Sometimes they are intimidated by stronger personalities and will not risk hurting others' feelings by not inviting them on the team. They want everyone to be happy, but long-term harmony is often sacrificed for short-term peace.

A third reason is that the planter has limited time. This is especially true if the planter is bivocational, subsidizing personal income with outside work. Life can be a pressure cooker of balancing competing interests. The time-strapped church planter may not naturally exercise care in choosing leaders. And, frankly, he or she is happy that at least someone wants to serve and lift some of the leadership burden away.

A fourth reason for disharmony is that some leaders were not allowed to lead in previous church experiences, so this is their opportunity to become key influencers. No one, including planters/pastors, has entirely pure motives, but on some occasions there are those whose motives are blatantly impure.

A final reason that new church leadership boards may be conflict-ridden is that assumptions are made that the initial leaders will be the perpetual leaders. When disharmony or other issues arise, it is only with great pain that leaders are asked or forced to leave the team. There is no "clean" way to leave a leadership team or to remove someone from a leadership team.

Experience shows that it is possible both to meet the leadership need of a new church and avoid the pitfalls referenced above. The solution is based on at least four principles:

1) There must be multiple leadership phases before a formal board is chosen;

2) There must be an avoidance of church-sounding nomenclature as these leadership teams are formed;

3) There must be a clear purpose and timeframe for each phase;

4) There must be a "changing of the guard" at each phase.

As an example, during the launch team phase of the new church, a major mistake a church planter could make would be to "appoint elders." Rather, the planter should adhere to the above principles and create a temporary team called (perhaps) the Launch-Team Advisory Board, whose purpose is to help the church planter make significant decisions while this church is growing its team and preparing to launch public services. Not all members need to come from the new church plant. Trusted leaders from a parent church or from another community can play a valued role. Participants are told clearly (in writing) that they are being invited to help the planter make important leadership decisions up until the time the church is launched publicly. After the church is public, the Launch-Team Advisory Board will be dissolved, and a new team will rise up to take its place.

Following the launch, a new entity, perhaps the Transitional Advisory Group, or "TAG-Team," is formed. Over the next few weeks the planter will prayerfully consider formulating a new leadership team to take the church to the next level. Some from the former board will be invited to participate, but others will step aside and make room for newcomers. This is a good time to add some "specialists" to the team: people with skills and interests in writing, theology, documentation, organization, and so on. It is during this phase that the Constitution, Statement of Faith, and formal leadership structure should be clearly defined, written, and adopted. The planter then prayerfully decides who should stay, who should step aside, and which newcomers should be invited to participate in TAG-Team, which will help the planter make important leadership decisions during the first year of the new church's life.

This pattern repeats as often as necessary until the formal board is chosen, perhaps an elder or deacon structure. By this time, enough history has transpired for the planter and the leaders of the church to have a pretty good idea of who should work with whom, and who might be best suited for a formal leadership role with a longer commitment. Many of the value and agenda harmony issues have been resolved, and a number of other benefits have been achieved–not the least of which is that the church has started to model that leaders come and go, and that no one is indispensable. Church planter Terry Martell advises that, as a general rule, it is better to assign people to jobs rather than to roles. "Roles" connotes titles and policy making, but "jobs" connotes service. Once a "role" is given away, it can be difficult to take it back if necessary.

This multiphase leadership template works well in small towns. To legislate against Post-Launch Syndrome, Mike Evans of New Richmond, Wis. (population 4,500) conducted a launch team funeral at a local mortuary. Launch team members came with their written memories, which were encased in a time capsule, to be unearthed on the launch day of Faith Community Church's first daughter church. Members were also given a handcrafted serving tray as a gift and as a reminder that their purpose now was to serve.

In the beginning days of launch team development the "early adopters" come on board with great vision and enthusiasm but sometimes without perseverance, leadership skills, or proven character. They can be very helpful, but most will not move on to the next leadership phase. Utilizing multiple leadership phases helps move them out of leadership into another area of service. Additional phases allow the church planter to add some late adopters to the Leadership Team while moving other leaders. Also, as the church moves towards the public launch, the Launch Team will expand, so having a second stage allows the freedom and flexibility to add new leaders who have come on board since the first leadership phase.

General benefits to following this approach include: modeling flexibility in leadership, modeling that leadership is service, providing greater flexibility in identifying and slotting leaders, assimilating and incorporating new leaders with ease (keeping power-brokers to a minimum), involving godly and gifted women without a great deal of theological struggle, and discerning God's leadership choices prayerfully.

EVANGELISM AND OUTREACH

The second major post-launch issue which may suffer is evangelism and outreach. Ironically, the church which is being planted for the express purpose of outreach can succumb to inward pressure to manage infrastructure and to perform weekend services. Specific efforts must be implemented to keep evangelism and outreach at the forefront of the church's activity. This is where the small town church plant has a strategic advantage over the one in the city. To begin, the natural relational webs that exist in smaller communities lend themselves toward evangelism. As the new church is legitimized, its activities become drawing points for those who are curiously seeking spiritual fulfillment. In the smaller town or rural area a small amount of creativity looks incredibly unique and relevant compared to usual church activity, and the costs involved in getting the word out are nominal. There are at least three spheres where evangelism and outreach can take place: target ministries, service projects/community involvement, and seeker services.

Target ministries in a small town can be varied and unique. One new church implemented, very early on, a Mothers of Preschoolers program for those raising small children. It was easily advertised by word of mouth and local media, and became a major outreach vehicle. On the men's side, church planter Gary Rohrmayer of Oconomowoc, Wis. understood that hunting and fishing are important cultural realities in small communities. He instituted routine Wild Game Nights, where men would come together to exchange hunting and fishing stories while feasting on their game. Such attraction events often included a guest speaker, such as a professional fisherman, who would also share his testimony in Christ. This particular event led to men's retreats and Bible studies. Children's ministries, youth groups, twelve-step recovery groups, and the like all have possibilities. In all likelihood, other existing churches in town have overlooked such creative outreach opportunities, giving the new church an untapped ministry field by meeting legitimate needs among the unchurched.

Service projects and other forms of community involvement can also be an effective way for the new church to engage itself in evangelism and outreach. Bob Marsh, church planter in Mayville, Wis. (population 4,500) mobilized his new church to systematically clean as many windshields as possible of the cars parked in town for Mayville Days. Not only did this create a positive predisposition toward the new church, but it gave the members genuine contact with the community at large. When the church I planted participated in a food drive for a community food pantry, members made a statement by contacting a large food distributorship to purchase dented cans and torn packages of food for a fraction of the price. The result was a public relations hit, with local media touting the new church for its concern. During its infancy, members of Grace Fellowship Church of Cortez, Colo. (population 7,000) donated labor and funds to build a playground in a needy area, reinforcing their commitment to compassionate outreach. When the brand new Faith Community Church of New Richmond, Wis. organized a short-term missions trip to assist an orphanage in the Ukraine, members gave generously to see that the venture would be successful. Although such a service project, being overseas, did not directly lead to increased membership for the church, the project levied against post-launch syndrome in two important ways: it instilled the value of evangelism, outreach and compassion in its members, and it contributed to positive community goodwill by being recognized as a church which truly cared. Bob Hughes, who planted the musically talented Riverwood Community Church of Burlington, Wis. organizes a float each year for Burlington's Chocolate Days parade. The parade includes the Riverwood worship band, displaying for all to see that Riverwood is a contemporary and fun-loving church.

This highlights one fact of small town life: there is almost always some sort of annual festival that celebrates some unique aspect of the community. There is a parade, a fun run, live music, a beer tent and maybe an eating contest to devour whatever cuisine the locality is known for. New Hope Evangelical Free Church in Cedaredge, Colo. takes a key role each year in "Applefest," sponsoring music groups and hosting a booth with free refreshments, literature, and a sign-up for raffle items such as Bibles and music CDs which provides a follow-up contact list for interested people. It would be a mistake for a new church in any small community to ignore its town's festival.

A third way for new churches in smaller communities to overcome a drop in evangelism and outreach is to strategically plan and capitalize on seeker-oriented worship services during the most opportune times of the year. Remembering the three-humped camel template, which illustrates two or three seasons in the calendar life of a community which make for more effective church outreach, new churches in smaller communities can make special efforts to attract newcomers. Rick Warren states that the key way to build an evangelism culture is to increase visitor flow to the church.

> Increasing the size of your church does not require the intelligence of a rocket scientist: You must simply get more people to visit! No one becomes a church member without first being a visitor. If you only have a few visitors each year, you'll have even fewer new members. A crowd is not a church, but to grow a larger church you must first attract a crowd.
>
> What is the most natural way to increase the number of visitors to your church? By making members feel guilty for not inviting friends? No. By putting up a big sign that says "Visitors Welcome"? No. By

cold-calling on homes in your community? Probably not. By holding attendance contests? Unlikely. By using telemarketing or advertising? Wrong again.

The answer is quite simple: Create a service that is intentionally designed for your members to bring their friends to. And make the service so attractive, appealing, and relevant to the unchurched that your members are eager to share it with the lost people they care about.[52]

With a welcoming environment, relevant music, a helpful message, and all of the other elements of a seeker-oriented or seeker-sensitive series, the small town church has ample opportunity to keep growing. Again, the smaller market church plant has a strategic advantage at this point for at least two reasons.

First, any degree of creativity or innovation is amplified because, compared to what other churches are doing, it will be viewed as incredibly creative. In addition to the standard elements which can bring creativity to a service (drama, good music, video presentations, and so on) there are other methodologies which always play well in a small town. One such method is to have a well-known celebrity as a guest at the service—and in a smaller community the definition of "celebrity" is broader than in a metropolitan area. Christian athletes at the college and professional levels are always a hit. One church planter invited an Olympic gold medal wrestler to give his testimony and host a wrestling clinic for budding athletes after the service. The event was a huge success. Television personalities from the nearby stations work well, too. In the church that I planted a sportscaster from a metropolitan television station came for our five-year anniversary service to give his testimony, again with great success. At such services it is important that the celebrity's portion of the service is limited to a few minutes. He or she should not bring the morning message, since that is an opportunity for the church planter to showcase his or her public speaking abilities. I recommend that the pastor maintain control of the microphone and interview the celebrity rather than give the guest unbridled reign of the timeline. It is also helpful if such an event is at the front end of the series to serve as a kickoff event that will entice attendees to come back again.

Creativity usually pays off in the small market. One new church that had a weak music ministry routinely hosted a "band month." There are usually decent up-and-coming Christian bands somewhere in the area who are looking for places to show their talents. Or established churches will loan out their band for a Sunday. By lining up bands for four or five weeks in a row a truly exciting atmosphere can be created. Not only

[52]Warren, *The Purpose-Driven Church*, 252-253.

does it provide momentum and give the regular musicians a break, but it showcases to the church and to the community the direction in which the new church is headed. And momentum can be capitalized in some distinct ways. Seasoned church planters in smaller communities know that a children's Christmas program should always be held during the regular service time–not at an alternative time. Every momentum event should showcase the church as it normally is–creative, upbeat, and welcoming. New churches should also not neglect the value of anniversaries: six month, one year, two year, and so on. Each becomes a chance (or an excuse) to do something momentous and thus draw newcomers into the fold.

The second advantage that smaller market church plants have in creating a seeker-oriented series is that it does not cost much to get the word out. Though Rick Warren rightly argues that advertising isn't the key to church growth, the case can still be made that use of the local media, especially in a smaller market, only legitimizes what the new church is about and cultivates the receptivity level of residents. Flyers, newspaper articles, direct mail, and all of the other tools mentioned earlier can help push the seeker series in front of potential attendees.

A mistake that church planters commonly make is that they give up on marketing and outreach efforts if it does not appear to instantly create a visitor flow. As one experienced planter remarked, "People quit advertising once it doesn't work once." Such church planters erroneously think that the only time for marketing is at the launch of the church. A specific and intentional marketing strategy to augment the efforts put into the seeker-oriented weekend series gives parishioners the backup support they need to invite potential churchgoers. With every step bathed in prayer and dependence on God, a powerful combination for outreach can be forged.

Obviously, drawing newcomers to a church service is only the beginning of an intentional assimilation and discipleship program. But even in a small community people generally assimilate by first bonding with the pastor, then bonding with the church, and ultimately bonding with the Lord of the church, Jesus. These proven methods of outreach serve new churches well in their post-launch phases by setting a genetic code of evangelism and outreach to carry them through the years.

PART THREE: CREATING A MOVEMENT BY STARTING SMALL

Chapter 8: Regional and Denominational Strategies

THE ROAD TO THE CITY STARTS IN THE SMALL TOWN

Since the mid-1980s, in part due to the work of the now defunct Fuller Institute of Church Growth, denominational leaders in North America have embraced the planting of new churches as an important part of their evangelism and expansion efforts. In many cases church planting was seen as the obvious choice for denominational rebirth. My own denomination was caught up in this as well, with leaders asserting that there would be no future for our fellowship of churches if new churches were not planted. Each year net losses of churches that had died natural deaths showed up on the annual statistical report. But with no new churches listed to offset the downward trend, it was a losing battle.

As a result of the mid-80s resurgence, denomination after denomination adopted faith-stretching goals, returning to their roots as catalytic church planting movements. Or so they hoped. With visionary enthusiasm, goals were set, slogans were adopted, videos were edited, and brochures were printed. In fact, this was good. It was positive momentum such as this that attracted me, as a budding church planter, to move ahead with my denomination. The publicly adopted goal was to have 150 new churches in five years with the emphasis being on metropolitan areas. It seemed like vision to me, so I joined the effort.

It is natural that denominations would emphasize larger communities because, simply, that is where the greater population base and the greater potential harvest is located. That emphasis was established in the mid-1980s, and it still exists today. However, I am willing to challenge the notion that larger communities ought to be the first target for denominations and sending agencies that are just beginning to start new churches. Their greater payoff at the early stages will be with smaller communities, with incremental steps toward places of larger populations. In addition to the reasons I stated earlier, there is another critical reason that I advocate this position: momentum building. The challenge that regional leaders face when engineering a denomination-wide or district-wide church planting movement from scratch is that inertia is rampant. There is subtle and not-so-subtle resistance to the initiative, partly based on history and partly based on unknown fears. "We tried to plant churches before, and they were financial sinkholes." "We should empha-size church revitalization, and when our churches are healthy then we will start new churches." And so on. In this context, the worst thing a regional group could do is to attempt a church plant in a highly resistant area. Failures will set back any church planting movement for years to come. The days of planting churches in riskier, higher resistance areas will come, but not quite yet. Positive momentum with a trustworthy, measured track record must precede a roll of the dice. This is what Wal-Mart knows about church planting.

Denomination leaders and their constituents tend to keep score one church at a time. The size of church or kingdom-impact is noted, but not as much as the simple fact that the church exists. In other words, a district of 100 churches with a constituency of 15,000 people appears to be larger (presumably more noteworthy) than a district of 75 churches with 18,000 constituents. The point is this: the greatest psychological "win" for a district or denomination is another new church. Conversely, the greatest "loss" is for a church to cease to exist. With that being true, denominational strategists who wish to initiate church planting movements must capitalize on momentum wherever possible. They will be wise at first to plant churches where it is easiest, for the momentum payoff to their constituency will be sooner and more pronounced.

A case in point is Mission Wisconsin, the church extension (planting) arm of the Free Methodist Church in that state. I have consulted with this group to help them begin a church planting movement. As of this writing, this group has many of the systems in place that will allow them to build a multiplying and reproducing movement, so they are now begin-ning to target certain communities and recruit potential planters. It is critical, in my opinion, that this group of eleven churches gain a healthy "win" for their constituency right away. Without my prompting, the group naturally assumed that their first target should be a major popula-tion area, such as Milwaukee. They have now revisited this thought and are looking first at a smaller community which could give them a better chance at success. If their first new church succeeds, it will allow for numbers two, three, and four to be birthed sooner. In the vernacular of the gambler, we come to the table with a certain amount of poker chips. It is not wise to bet the house the first time into the game. When a greater number of chips are amassed, the riskier ventures will be warranted.

Another factor for leaders of a newly emerging church planting movement to consider—which may levy in favor of targeting smaller communities at the offset—is the history, psyche, and personality of the denomination. Many denominations, though not all by any means, have a rural or small town history. This is certainly true of my denomination, which traces its history to Swedish immigrant farmers who settled in the northcentral United States. Denominations and districts will do well to self-analyze their genetic code. If they are by history a rural/small town organization, they will be wise to avoid the natural sentiment to target a metropolitan area at first "because we don't have a church there," in favor of choosing a smaller community. At least some semblance of sociological affinity will exist with that smaller community, and perhaps even a bit of historical sentimentality can be capitalized on to get the work started.

Additionally, let me say a brief word regarding cross-cultural church planting. Leaders of new church planting movements need to exercise extreme care when first venturing to target other cultural and language groups in their geographical domain. To be sure, there is significant sentimentality in many cases to consider other cultural groups, and eventually these groups need to be targeted. But not yet. These will come when a track record of success has already been established. There are too many unknowns, and with church planting systems not yet mature in the dominant culture it is unlikely that transference can occur to another culture. My observation is that denominational leaders, under self-imposed pressures to "get another church" started, often lower the requirements and expectations for other cultural groups. Many times these can appear to be golden opportunities, without great financial cost or risk, and the constituency will sentimentally embrace the venture. Besides, the situation "just came to us," so the other costly up-front recruitment and assessment costs are never expended. But at this point the movement cannot afford the risk. Short-term gain often results in long-term pain.

The denominational predisposition to prefer larger communities to smaller ones when beginning church planting must be challenged. This is especially true in the early days when leaders carefully measure risks and do everything possible to capitalize on momentum.

DEVELOPING THE WILL FOR PLANTING CHURCHES
IN SMALLER COMMUNITIES

Leaders of church planting movements who overlook small towns or rural areas are ignoring wonderful mission opportunities and may be, in fact, disobedient to the Great Commission. And in the case of those new movements that are just getting underway, failure to capitalize on the opportunity of smaller communities may mean missing the chance to hone systems in a friendly environment. It is not only necessary, it is wise, to prioritize the targeting of smaller towns in any church planting master plan.

The prioritization of smaller communities must begin with movement leadership who should ponder the unreached markets in their geographical domain and make room for them in their strategic plan. Christian philosopher Francis Schaeffer, whose ministry center was in rural Switzerland, reflected on the importance of place and size by stating:

> Nowhere more than in America are Christians caught up in the twentieth-century syndrome of size. Size will show success. If I am consecrated, there will necessarily be large quantities of people, dollars, etc. This is not so. Not only does God not say that size and spiritual power go together, but he even reverses this (especially in the teaching of Jesus) and tells us to be deliberately careful not to choose a place too big for us. We all tend to emphasize big works and big places, but all such emphasis is of the flesh. To think in such terms is simply to hearken back to the old, unconverted, egoist, self-centered me.[59]

Leaders of church planting movements can gain spiritual passion for communities of all sizes by exposing themselves to regional demographics. Census Bureau information is readily available through government services and on the Internet. There is a good chance that volunteers can be enlisted to initiate the effort. The project should take a sound look at demographic trends and population data as it relates to smaller communities and rural areas. Who lives there? For how long? What macrotrends are noticeable? Besides the obvious information sources, much help can be gleaned from sociologists in regional colleges and universities who are often eager to share their knowledge. Coordination with other denominations with the purpose of sharing data about specific regions can lead to a broader understanding of the regional needs and opportunities. Population and demographic trends should be compared with church attendance statistics. Some areas may be consid-

---

[53]Francis Schaeffer, *A Christian View of Spirituality* (Westchester, Ill.: Crossway, 1982), 9.

ered oversaturated by some denominational groups, and it would be polit-
ically unpopular for them to forge new works there. But the same area
may be ripe for another group, without the hassle of internal opposition.

The growth of smaller communities and the Rural Rebound effect in
the United States should be helpful to leaders of church planting
movements as they prioritize church planting sites. But in order for this
direction to truly be embraced, leaders need to develop a spiritual passion
for such places. Jesus demonstrated such passion when he gazed upon
Jerusalem. "O Jerusalem, Jerusalem, you who kill the prophets and stone
those sent to you, how often I have longed to gather your children
together, as a hen gathers her chicks under her wings, but you were not
willing" (Matt. 23:37, NIV). The Apostle Paul effused spiritual passion for
specific people groups when he wrote, "I speak the truth in Christ–I am
not lying, my conscience confirms it in the Holy Spirit–I have great
sorrow and unceasing anguish in my heart. For I could wish that I myself
were cursed and cut off from Christ for the sake of my brothers, those of
my own race, the people of Israel" (Rom. 9:1-4, NIV). Though statistical
analysis and academic realities may play a part in moving leaders toward
action, there is no substitute for spiritual passion from the Holy Spirit to
bring concern for the lost.

CASTING VISION AND MOVING TOWARD IMPLEMENTATION

Denominational and district executives who wish to see their church
planting efforts jump-started need to cast vision to their constituency.
In the case of those who have no recent history of planting churches,
opposition to the vision will usually be quelled with statistical information and the need for planting new churches. In addition to the information provided earlier, leaders can include the following in their reports.

- Between 3,500 and 4,000 churches close their doors annually in the
  United States, while only 1,000 to 1,500 churches are started.

- In the United States, churches lose approximately 2.7 million people
  each year.

- The United States is the third largest mission field in the world, with
  at least 195 million people who are untouched by the gospel.

- North America is the only continent on earth where Christianity is
  not growing.

- No county in the United States has seen even a 1 percent church
  attendance increase in the last ten years.

- One study indicates that in churches that are fewer than three years
  old it takes three attendees to reach one person for Christ. In
  churches that are three to ten years old it takes seven attendees to

reach one person for Christ. In churches that are over ten years old it takes 89 attendees to reach one person for Christ.

• A Gallup survey indicates that 44 percent of Americans were unchurched in 1988. Peter Wagner sets the figure at 55 percent in 1990 and George Barna predicted a figure of 65 percent by the year 2000.[54]

Disseminating the information to justify a comprehensive church planting effort is just one part of vision casting, but it is an important part. Coupled with impassioned biblical and historical teaching, leaders can effectively move denominations that have been stagnant in planting new churches to mobilize money, prayer, and manpower to begin the task. Strategic thinking suggests that smaller communities be prioritized with these initial efforts, giving regional agencies their greatest potential for early victories. Success brings the momentum necessary to propel these agencies toward other necessary but more difficult target groups, such as those in urban environments.

In the case of a denomination or district which has attempted church planting with limited success, the vision-casting effort becomes more diffi-cult. Critics will argue that enough money and effort have been spent with little to show for it. However, leadership must stay the course, learn from its mistakes, and try again. Only success will overcome the negative momentum of initial failures. Such leaders will want to steer clear of hype but stand firm in their convictions that their movement is maturing and inching toward days when success will be more common than failure. This type of backlash is not uncommon. In fact, there are several phases that newly engineered church planting movements can expect to go through on their way toward proficiency.

THE SEVEN PHASES OF A CHURCH PLANTING MOVEMENT

Those responsible for seeing that new churches are planted often struggle to see their dreams fulfilled. Somewhere in their tenure they have embraced the truth that they must plant new churches. They have come to this conclusion for theological reasons and for pragmatic reasons as well. Churches have a natural life span. They come and they go; they live and they die. Without new churches the kingdom of God does not advance, and without new churches the denomination or district will not last for long. In my own denomination declining church numbers and the failure to plant new churches caused one prominent delegate to the 1984 annual meeting to ask with chilling rhetoric, "Do we have a future?" For most denominational leaders, success is measured by the number of churches under their care. Church planting has become a

---

[54]Current Thoughts and Trends, Carol Stream, IL, May, 1997.

priority. But leaders do struggle to see their dreams fulfilled. Once convinced that the planting of new churches must become a priority a typical scenario unfolds. Unfortunately, many groups stumble into church planting without a great deal of planning. When that happens we can expect up to seven phases to transpire before they become proficient in planting churches.

PHASE 1: LEADERSHIP ACQUIESCENCE AND VISION

In the first phase, Leadership Acquiescence and Vision, some people at the top of the organization embrace the reality that new churches must be planted. They have read literature, attended seminars, and been exposed to success stories of new churches and changed lives somewhere else. The pragmatic truth that newer "franchises" are needed to sustain the organization may also play a part. Casual discussions among the leaders coalesce into formal discussions and enthusiasm. Because denominational leaders "keep score" by the number of churches they superintend a strong conviction attends the thinking. It is not unusual for an exploratory committee or task force to be assigned the job of considering a target location and finding a church planter to start the work. In some organizations there is a cross-cultural linkage to the enthusiasm. There may be a sense that the denomination or district is too heterogeneous, and something must be done to help reach out to other races or cultural groups. Unless there is a parent church which is driving this vision, denominational leaders usually make their first few church plant decisions along geographical considerations, opting for locations where the denomination is underrepresented. With a good concentration of churches on the east side of the district it is reasoned that the natural place to start this new work is on the west side of the district. One additional advantage is that resistance levels will be lower since the likelihood that their established churches or pastors will be threatened is diminished.

PHASE 2: PROMOTION AND CONSTITUENT ENTHUSIASM

Following on the heels of the first phase of the initial vision comes Promotion and Constituent Enthusiasm. The constituency consists, in most cases, of the pastors, churches, and other stakeholders of the district and denomination. Since the support of the churches will be necessary for the venture to succeed, denominational leaders must do what they can to garner a positive predisposition for the project. Newsletters, prayer cards, and other printed materials announce the project. If the plan is for just one new church start, the promotional effort will obviously focus on that location and/or cultural group. In most cases the promotion for one new church start will flow with relative ease. If, however, the inaugural vision calls for something more aggressive such as multiple church plants or a church planting mission, the effort to gain constituent acceptance will be exponential. More than one denomination or district has stalled their future productivity by prematurely announcing an aggressive plan which disintegrates in due time.

It is during this season, when church planting is a novelty, that enthusiasm runs high. Financial and prayer support are generously contributed by churches. Established churches and pastors are glad to be part of a movement which is expanding the kingdom of God. There may be some cynics and skeptics, but the momentum is in favor of the plant beginning. The first few church planters and their families are adopted with ease, as part of the denominational family.

PHASE 3: INITIAL IMPLEMENTATION

Next, the project begins to be implemented. In the case of the singular church plant this means that a site is selected, a target group articulated, and a church planter chosen for the task. The church planter is relocated, and the project is underway. In some cases, a preexisting group awaits the arrival of the planter. Sometimes this works out well, but often this becomes problematic for the planter when varying value and agenda disharmony is discovered.

Inexperienced denominational leadership can make mistakes with any of these variables, but that is all part of the maturation process for the new movement. Should the first church plant begin effectively, the movement enjoys a window of opportunity with its constituency to work toward the next church plant and the other ones to follow. After general manager Ron Wolfe led the Green Bay Packers to victory in Super Bowl XXXI he reflected on how much momentum matters in changing the fabric of an organization. "You come in and say you have a plan, but honest to goodness you don't have a plan. You are just hoping to win some games and get some people off of your backs, to buy us some time and to structure the entire team the way you want it to be structured."[55] This is where one of the most curious realities of denominational life rears its head. Either the success or failure of the new season of church planting leads to the fourth phase: Constituent Backlash.

PHASE 4: CONSTITUENT BACKLASH

Constituent Backlash occurs when people of influence begin to make noise and raise suspicions about the newly developing church planting movement, often resulting in overt criticism of the leaders and polariza-

---

[55]Green Bay *Press Gazette*, 13 April 1997.

tion of the stakeholders. When church plant failures have accumulated, the criticism comes in the form of stewardship woes. The leadership of the movement will be second-guessed for having spent God's money on poorly devised ventures. A retreatist mentality will echo: we have waded into the waters of church planting; now we must race back to the shore of business as usual.

But not all or even most Constituent Backlash comes on the heels of church plant failures. Surprisingly to some, a good deal of criticism comes when church plants begin to succeed, often beyond some established churches which have helped fuel the movement financially. Criticism varies, but most centers on denominational loyalty or faithfulness to doctrinal minutiae. As an example, should a new church have a generic name which does not specify the denomination in the title, this becomes fodder for criticism. Also, in the event that a new church grows substantially but does not begin to participate in the denominational or district activities (stewardship, camping programs, retreats, meetings, and so on), there is a tendency to castigate the movement as a whole. Some stakeholders who were quiet up until then say that they had agreed to the procreation of new churches, but not these kind of churches.

PHASE 5: REEVALUATION AND LEARNING

The denominational or district undertaking which had embarked with such vision must now navigate turbulent waters, which leads to the fifth phase of maturity, Reevaluation and Learning. At a certain point, leadership queries themselves and others regarding their haphazard success rate or their public relations problems. Lessons are learned about the systems necessary to see an ongoing church planting movement develop. Leadership learns about selection of church planting candidates, risk factors involved in the mobilization of qualified candidates, the expectations which the denomination has of its church planters and the church planters may have of their denomination. They learn the importance of coaching church planters effectively to succeed, the significance of spiritual dynamics, the support of spouses and families, and a host of other issues that had never been considered up until then. Groups that have attempted a failed cross-cultural church plant because it seemed easier or carried a sentimental pull, think through the necessity of objective systems. Books, literature, and experts may be consulted. Seminars may be attended in order to evaluate what has happened so as to create a better framework for the future of this church planting movement.

Denominational leadership also learns lessons on public relations with their constituents. They discover that some criticism cannot be avoided, but they also discover that there are better ways to enlist the support of a suspicious electorate. This newfound humility can be helpful in propelling the movement. If failed church plants have been routine up until now, there may be an increased call to prayer and dependency upon God. But if success has been the precedent, leadership also learns to proceed with humility that honors both new and established churches as valued works of God.

PHASE 6: SYSTEMS IMPLEMENTATION

The biggest lesson learned in Phase Five is that there must be routine and reliable structures in place to sustain a movement. Phase Six, then, refers to Systems Implementation. Leaders who are accustomed to quick fixes will find this season of maturation to be arduous, but in due time the payoff becomes evident. Indeed, they have no logical choice. It may be that it was their prior impetuousness that led to some degree of disintegration. Systems Implementation, or the "Turn-Key Revolution," involves the slow process of developing routine ways to accomplish tasks with minimal acceptable standards of achievement.

Business theorist Michael Gerber outlines five rules which govern the Turn-Key Revolution, which allows for maximum proficiency of branch franchises. 1) The model will be operated by people with the lowest possible level of skill. It will not be dependent on superstars, but on good people working within the framework of excellent systems. 2) The model will stand out as a place of impeccable order. There will be few surprises because there will be routine methods of accomplishing tasks. 3) All work in the model will be documented in operations manuals. The oral tradition of doing business will give way to a written tradition that outlines procedures, eliminating guesswork. 4) The model will provide a uniformly predictable service to the consumer. Consumers will be better served by the enterprise because they will not be caught off-guard or be surprised with the way in which they are treated. 5) The model will utilize a uniform color, dress, and facilities code. Detail will be given to the way in which the organization presents itself and engenders confidence from those who are related to it.[56]

A number of systems need to be developed in order for a church planting movement to mature and expand, including spiritual dynamics, recruitment of church planters, assessment of potential planters, training, coaching of church planters, established church involvement, and funding. All of these will be explored in chapter 9. The most important thing to notice here, however, is that if leadership begins a movement by prioritizing systems development, much unnecessary heartache can be avoided.

---

[56]Michael E. Gerber, *The E Myth* (New York: Harperbusiness, 1986) 58-67.

Many advantages of having a systems approach rather than a haphazard approach to the planting of churches are apparent. First, the guesswork about who, where, when, and how is stripped away because now there are standard operating procedures. Second, it allows for a broader based ownership of the church planting movement among the constituency because systems require more participants taking small parts in the mission. Third, it gives leadership greater opportunity to lead strategically by freeing up time to do just that. Fourth, a systems approach is not personality dependent. The mission can outlive the initial visionary because the structures are in place and perpetuate themselves. A solid biblical example is found during the early days of the New Testament church.

> In those days when the number of disciples was increasing, the Grecian Jews among them complained against the Hebraic Jews because their widows were being overlooked in the daily distribution of food. So the Twelve gathered all the disciples together and said, "It would not be right for us to neglect the ministry of the word of God in order to wait on tables. Brothers, choose seven men from among you who are known to be full of the Spirit and wisdom. We will turn this responsibility over to them and will give our attention to prayer and the ministry of the word."
>
> This proposal pleased the whole group. They chose Stephen, a man full of faith and of the Holy Spirit; also Philip, Procorus, Nicanor, Timon, Parmenas, and Nicolas from Antioch, a convert to Judaism. They presented these men to the apostles, who prayed and laid their hands on them.
>
> So the word of God spread. The number of disciples in Jerusalem increased rapidly, and a large number of priests became obedient to the faith. (Acts 6:1-7, NIV)

Commenting on this text, Richard Longenecker contends that systems can bring greater participation and productivity.

> And even when the church found it necessary to divide internal responsibilities and assign different functions, the early believers saw these as varying aspects of one total ministry. The early church seems to have been prepared to adjust its procedures, alter its organizational structure, and develop new posts of responsibility in response to existing needs and for the sake of the ongoing proclamation of the Word of God.[57]

---

[57]Richard N. Longenecker, *The Acts of the Apostles*, vol. 9 of *The Expositor's Bible Commentary*, ed. Frank E. Gaebelein (Grand Rapids: Zondervan, 1984), 331.

When a new church planting movement reaches this stage of Systems Implementation it has come to the point of frustration, but it is unwilling to give up its mission. Reasoning that there must be some way to plant churches effectively, the leadership is willing to take the time to build a strong foundation. One challenge for denominational or district leaders during the Systems Implementation phase is to convince the constituency that this effort is worth it. Productivity will appear to have evaporated if no churches are being planted during this season. Good leadership assures the stakeholders that this restructuring is necessary to avoid repeating the mistakes of the past and to step into an era of effective productivity.

PHASE 7: PRODUCTIVITY AND MULTIPLICATION

Finally, a church planting movement has truly begun. Phase seven, Productivity and Multiplication, speaks of a mature movement which has functional systems led by competent people. Churches are now being planted with less hype but more productivity than before. Rather than just adding a few new churches here and there, many without success, the agency is now watching multiplication occur with strong rates of success.

This does not mean that the movement will not have struggles or challenges. Maturity does not mean the absence of troubles, but it does mean that there are normal procedures in place to address problems. There will be breakdowns in systems which will need to be addressed. There will be new systems to be implemented when ministry aspirations eclipse known resources. There will be personnel changes and disappointments. There may be a rebound effect among the constituency (churches, pastors, and members) who were at one time critical of failures but are now feeling neglected by the positive perception of the church planting movement. However, the momentum will be positive, the constituency will be glad for the most part, and the kingdom of God will be advancing.

Chapter 9: Taking a Systems Approach

The previous chapter describes how movements naturally seem to evolve into systems. But what if we traded in an "evolutionary" approach for "creationism," and we started a church planting movement intentionally? If we did that we would be taking a systems approach from the very beginning. Once leaders are convinced that they must create excellent systems in order for their church planting movement to multiply, succeed, and perpetuate, they can begin the architectural groundwork necessary to build a sustainable future. There are literally dozens of systems we could implement, but I emphasize seven in particular: spiritual dynamics, established church involvement, coaching, recruitment, funding, assessment, and training. In this chapter I'd like to unpack what those systems might look like, and in chapter 10 I'll make some suggestions on how and where to begin.

SPIRITUAL DYNAMICS

Leaders of church planting movements should cast a curious eye toward the underevangelized small towns and rural areas under their care, asking what may be behind the lack of Christian witness in those communities. Some leaders know what it is like to see church planting attempts fail once, twice, and three times in one location—but often they look first to the human or sociological dimensions for answers to their frustration, rather than the unseen world. But when we take spiritual dynamics seriously and arrange for prayer systems to develop regional prayer emphases, good things can and do happen. According to one report, after 25 years of ineffective ministry in India, OMS International decided to recruit 1,000 people to pray 15 minutes each day for regional church planting efforts. "The results were startling. In just a few years the work grew from 25 churches with 2,000 believers to 550 churches with more than 73,000 believers."[58]

In short, a spiritually sensitive church planting movement continues to ask the questions, "What are we missing by not seeking God?" and "What might we gain when we do?". Henry Blackaby's popular book, *Experiencing God*, speaks of this type of thinking as "working where God is working." "To live a God-centered life, you must focus your life on God's purposes, not your own plans. You must seek from God's

---

[58]George Otis, *The Last of the Giants* (Grand Rapids: Chosen Books, 1991), 248.

perspective rather than from your own distorted human perspective."[59]
He applies that to church planting, too.

> Our church sensed that God wanted us to help start new churches all
> across Central and Western Canada. We had hundreds of towns and
> villages that had no evangelical church. To know where to start
> churches, some churches would start with a population study or
> survey. Then they would apply human logic to decide where the
> most promising and productive places might be. By now you know
> that I would take a different approach.
>   We tried to find out what God already was doing around us. We
> believed that He would show us where He was at work, and that
> revelation would be our invitation to join Him. We began praying
> and watching to see what God would do next in answer to our
> prayers. . . . [60]

Researcher George Otis says essentially the same thing. "Those who
take the time both to talk to and listen to God before launching their
ministry ventures will not only find themselves in the right place at the
right time, but they will also know what to do when they get there."[61]
John Dawson adds, "Wait on the Lord for insight. Don't rely on finite
reasoning or human cunning. Spiritual battles are won by following
revelation given by the Holy Spirit. If we listen to God with childlike
dependency, He will guide us into victory."[62]
    I have seen some creative and helpful strategies for spiritual dynamics
in regional church planting movements. Among these are intercession
teams, monthly prayer letters, e-mail prayer notices, regional concerts of
prayer for church planting, occasional 24-hour prayer initiatives, prayer
walking, the mobilization of retirees who are serious about prayer, organized prayer "strike teams" to welcome the arrival of new church planters,
prayer calendars, and creative prayer reminders. As an example, on my
refrigerator is a wipe-off memo board that was given to me by a start-up
church planting movement in Iowa. It says, "Pray for Iowa Church
Planting." So I do.

ESTABLISHED CHURCH INVOLVEMENT

When established churches are actively engaged in starting other
churches risks go way down and the possibility of success goes way up.
A quick look at the Risk Factor Analysis (appendix 1) shows that a

---

[59]Henry T. Blackaby and Claude V. King, *Experiencing God* (Nashville: Broadman and Holman, 1994), 65-66.
[60]Ibid., 76-77.
[61]C. Peter Wagner, *Breaking Strongholds in Your City* (Ventura, Calif.: Regal, 1993), 19.
[62]John Dawson, *Taking Our Cities for God* (Altamonte Springs, Fla.: Creation House, 1989), 171.

number of resources are available when other churches are involved, including funding sources, the potential number of launch team members, and the myriad of intangibles that having nearby churches that "really want you to succeed" can bring.

Since church planting success is greatly enhanced when a parent church is involved, it makes sense that district or denominational leaders encourage and promote established churches to become parent churches. The advantages for the district are many. For one, whatever budding animosity might exist between established and new churches is reduced. One prominent pastor in my own denomination has become renowned for his advocacy of church parenting. He has repeatedly stated publicly that his greatest regret is that it took him too long to experience the blessing of parenting. Such candid admonitions go a long way toward bridging the gap between newer churches and established ones. A corollary benefit to district church planting leadership is that when parenting occurs it creates a natural peer-based leadership core comprised of pastors who will influence others. Rather than district employees cheerleading the expansion of parenting, those who have waded into the reproduction waters become the chief proponents of the model. Churches that are hesitant to birth a new church find the challenge and encouragement of peers who have done so successfully to be powerfully motivational.

I know of at least two ways to help motivate established churches to be involved in a district-wide initiative. The first is to create a system that routinely challenges individual local churches to become parent churches. An excellent resource by Bob Logan and Steve Ogne, *Churches Planting Churches* (available from ChurchSmart Resources, St. Charles, Ill.), provides workbook instruction and a video challenge to prepare churches to start new works. Additionally, it suggests a delivery system called a Parent Church Network that brings pastors and leaders of potential parent churches together on a routine basis for training and accountability. The system works well, but in some cases it can be difficult to recruit pastors who are not already immersed in the church planting culture. I have seen many new and healthy churches started as a result of Parent Church Networks.

An alternative to a Parent Church Network is to bring pastors and leaders from a specific geographical area to cooperate together on a specific church plant. These coalitions spread the load of church planting to several churches. In my national TeAmerica work in my denomination we refer to these gatherings as LEAD Teams, the acronym referring to the four components of the 24-hour meeting: Learning, Encouraging, Achieving, and Dreaming. The idea is to create an environment for "relationships worth building and dreams worth chasing," so a good amount of the meeting is devoted to team building fun activities (golf, horseback riding, laser tag), personal sharing, and intercession. The LEAD Teams meet four to six times each year, and we are finding them to be excellent delivery systems that bring mutual encouragement for established church pastors while building a groundswell movement of regional church planting.

I have one final thought for the involvement of established churches as it relates to smaller town church planting. One major reason for potential parent churches or coalitions of established churches near smaller communities to consider these for their first daughter church: safety. An analogy comes from the birth process of my first son, Andrew. Lori was a hesitant mom, not longing to give birth and have babies like many women do. The birth event was a challenge, as most are. However, when the baby was born my wife was able to say within five minutes, "I could do that again." The parallel for parent churches is obvious. Many churches that could commit to starting daughter churches are hesitant to do so. They fear the worst, and they do so only out of obligation. If their first birth goes well, however, there is a better chance that the parent church will do it again. The idea is to maximize the parent church's potential: we would prefer that a family of daughter churches results, over time, rather than the birthing of a single church.

Safety matters a great deal to established churches who are just getting into the church planting game. Some churches would never parent in their own town, at least at the beginning of their parenting cycle, for fear of losing many people to the new, fresh church. But by planting in a neighboring community the parent churches avoid the possibility that there will be a mass exodus to the new church. Instead, there will most likely be some attendees at the parent church who are from the neighboring community, and most parent churches can absorb that loss. The established churches can then focus on providing short-term missionary help to the new church rather than watch large numbers leave permanently. While this is not the type of kingdom-oriented thinking which we would eventually like to see in a movement, it at least is a first step to advance the cause. Then, as the new birth goes well, the established churches may one day become so kingdom-oriented that they would even risk planting in their own community. From a strategic perspective, it positions that church to plant many more new churches if its first one or two go well. And things have a better chance of going well if the planting is done with minimal pain to the parent, especially in the beginning.

Often, while speaking at small town churches, I gather groups of people around highway maps and ask them to note communities within their county that are without an effective evangelical witness. At least in my part of the country, people are always able to name many small communities that are in need of a new church. Also, depending on the demographics of a region, a number of small town or rural churches can coalesce and work together to plant a church in an unreached community. Reminiscent of the Wal-Mart "stretch and fill" tactic, these churches make sure that prayer and personnel needs are covered for the new church plant. In one such coalition in our area the small town parent church received considerable help from its parent, grandparent, and great-grandparent churches. This four-generation matrix was comprised of churches all within fifty miles of each other, each with a relational link to the other, with very positive results. District leadership operates wisely when they look for ways to encourage church parenting from and toward smaller communities.

COACHING

Coaching is the hands-on process of helping others to succeed. In the context of ministry, a church planting coach is one who adds value to a new venture by offering strategic encouragement to planters. Observation and care is administered in at least three environments: the ministry field (concern that the new work is advancing), the personal life (individual development and relationship with God), and the coaching relationship (the interpersonal dynamic between the coach and planter). Just as in the athletic world where the best athletes are often coached the most, even the best church planters benefit greatly from good coaching.

Church planting movements must provide coaching for their church planters, and it must insure a way for qualified coaches to develop and be held accountable. A reliable coaching system brings incredible payoff. Church planters feel cared for and their projects are more successful. And in the case of church planters who are in smaller towns or rural areas (some of whom would not be qualified at this time to church plant in an urban or suburban realm) coaching is critical to their success, both personally and professionally. In my ministry, for instance, I estimate that only 20 percent of our church planters would survive and succeed without coaching, and even those benefit from the accountability and experience which coaching brings.

Again, the issue here is developing a coaching system. In my experience, coaching systems among denominations break down in one or more of three areas: recruitment, accountability, and quality control. When any of these is not managed properly, the likelihood is that coaching will be perfunctory and of questionable value. If these three areas are adequately addressed by movement leaders, coaching thrives.

The recruitment of good coaches or potential coaches makes or breaks a movement. When a new church planting movement is dawning, it is not uncommon for leaders to acquiesce to the concept of coaching, but mistakes are often made in the selection of those who might become coaches. One problem is that people who do not have the time or the willingness to learn are pursued. Sometimes these people are asked to be part of a coaching team in hopes that their participation will "win them" to the movement, but the results are predictably unfavorable. Movement leaders do better when they seek to recruit coaches who are mature, loyal, teachable, and willing to give the time necessary.

Potential coaches should be recruited with the expectation that, once approved and mobilized, they are responsible to meet monthly with their appointees and stay in touch by telephone and e-mail during the interim. Usually church planting coaches work with their planters through the first or second anniversary of the new church's launch. They can be given initial training through the use of resources such as *Empowering Leaders through Coaching* (which gives basic training in the art of coaching) and the *Church Planters' Toolkit* (which covers the basics of getting a new church started). In my work I lead introductory training events for new coaches called Coaching Quickstarts, which take place over a twenty-four hour period to reinforce the teaching in *Empowering Leaders through Coaching*.

The initial recruitment and training of church planting coaches is critical to the success of the movement, but if that is where the intentionality of movement leadership ends, there will be fallout along the way. "Coaching entropy," where coaches stray from their responsibilities, occurs unless coaches are held accountable. This entropy occurs not because of the inherent irresponsibility of coaches but because they are busy, enterprising individuals who have learned to multitask as a lifestyle. They may cut corners and not coach up to their potential. Movement leaders are mistaken if they think that once coaches are trained and mobilized they seamlessly carry out their jobs. So there must be some way to insure accountability. Movement leadership must require a reporting system and see that regular contact with their coaches takes place.

One way to bring about accountability is to have some sort of payoff for coaches for doing their jobs. In some contexts a small amount of pay helps to assure that this happens. When coaches move from the realm of being volunteers to being employees, movement leaders have a stronger leverage point in requiring faithfulness to the job. If this paradigm is adopted, leadership must be prepared for the day when expansion of the coaching staff eclipses salary resources. But some type of payoff can make a difference.

The best way to address quality control issues is to bring coaches together from time to time for training and accountability. This can involve studying classic and current information on church planting, testing one another, intercession, and creating an environment of "raising the bar" for the movement in general. A fuller explanation of how to do this is found in chapter 8 of *Empowering Leaders through Coaching*. I recommend that church planting coaches be brought together at least quarterly for some type of meeting that involves accountability and quality control.

The focus here is on system development. Movement leaders who envision an expanding, multiplying church planting organization should exercise care in the areas of recruitment, accountability, and quality control. They will mobilize a coaching team with camaraderie and expansion in mind. The payoff in terms of church planting success rates will be worth the effort.

RECRUITMENT

New church planting movements eventually need to start finding the people to plant the churches.

I have observed misunderstandings among denominational leaders when it comes to recruiting church planters. Most often leaders cite the lack of potential church planting candidates, as if they are elusive and incredibly difficult to find. This is a false assumption: there are many potential candidates, and they are not as difficult to find as some people think. The major issue is not finding them, but handling them properly when they are found. The second misunderstanding about recruitment is that it is a matter of trickery or deception in which the aggressors (in this case, the denomination or sponsoring agency) must leverage potential candidates to get them to succumb to the agenda at hand. In fact, this is a poor philosophical approach to recruitment because it assumes that the candidate would not be well served by pursuing a church planting venture. But God has gifted many people to do the job. I like to tell candidates, "I don't see myself as much as a recruiter as I do a scout. Recruiting sounds like talking someone into doing something they shouldn't do. I'm looking for people who should be planting churches."

When church planters are recruited from within an organization (established church pastors, youth pastors, and personal acquaintances), the process naturally becomes easier. Ground rules, expectations, and agenda issues are often already assumed. But when potential church planters come from outside of an organization, a much more intentional courtship process must take place. In such cases it is imperative that the sponsoring organization present itself professionally, with confidence, or they will quickly be ignored by potential candidates. Recruiters must realize that they are dealing with people's lives. When candidates believe that an organization knows what it is doing and is intentional in its procedures, there is a greater likelihood that they will give it a second look. Changing denominations or moving to another part of the country can be scary, but the draw of an organization that can help the planter succeed can be compelling.

Church planting organizations need to have a positive public posture. Written materials must be professional and coherent. One vehicle that seems to work well for many districts is a professionally designed church planting folder, which can then be filled with materials that accurately spell out the specific vision and services of the organization. Such folders should include a welcome letter, denominational distinctives, promotional material from tourist bureaus and the Chambers of Commerce, vision documents, and explanations of what steps are necessary to move from being casually interested to actually planting a church. References to the region's demographics, including specifics on smaller towns and rural areas (as well as larger communities), will open some candidates' eyes to new venues. A "frequently asked questions" sheet can eliminate some concerns the candidate may have. A good employment application with a signed waiver to contact references should be included. This is a true gauge of the candidates' interest in the organization, because if they bother to send in the application it shows that they serious about moving ahead—and are thus worth attention.

Professionalism in other ways makes a difference. The name of the organization can reflect a positive outlook for the planting of new churches. So can its logo. Up-front money to have something done professionally pays big dividends. An Internet web site does not need to be flashy, but it should look attractive. All of this creates an atmosphere of confidence for those considering a possible relationship with the organization.

There are many good ways to find potential candidates. However, I've found one of the worst and least efficient is the standard display at a seminary or Bible school. It may be worth trying, but compared to other methods available today, this should not play a prominent role in most organizations' candidate searches. The Internet is the best investment today. Many Christian institutions allow for free job placement advertisements. Some charge a monthly fee to advertise through their web sites or in their publications, but these can pay off substantially. The organization should develop some sort of web site for advertising purposes and register keywords such as "church planting," "small towns," and "rural" with search engines. Church planting can also be promoted within the district or denomination. Flyers can be sent, on occasion, to district pastors seeking referrals for potential church planter candidates. When names are received a follow-up mechanism should be triggered which involves sending out written materials, phone calls, and initial candidate assessment.

Interested candidates always ask, "Where are you targeting?" I find that the best response is to be evasive at this point, stating, "Just about everywhere." If target communities are within driving distance of the candidate or couple, they will be contacting the Chamber of Commerce before sundown and driving through prematurely. I do go on to explain that we take the candidates through a diagnostic process to match them to a community where they can succeed. It is at this point that I may bring up the idea of planting in a smaller community than the planter might have envisioned. It is important if small town church planting is a priority for the organization that potential planters realize that small town does not have to equate with "small church." Throughout the recruitment process I ask myself whether this person has the skill sets necessary to plant a church in an urban or suburban environment, or whether he or she would fit better in a less populated area.

A final component of the recruitment process is arranging meetings between church planters and those who will work with them. Candidates, and especially candidate couples, need to meet others who will be part of their church planting universe. If the movement has matured to the point that some seasoned and successful church planters are already doing the work, they can be included in the recruitment process. Meeting coaches and support staff over a meal can also take some of the unknowns out of the church planters' mind. Occasional attraction events, such as a regional training event or a church planting retreat, can help candidates experience the excitement of the movement. They can also provide interaction time with others who can share both the struggles and victories of the work. If the church planting organization has a spousal and family support ministry a representative can make an early contact with the family to help answer questions and alleviate concerns. This brings an incredible amount of security and legitimization to the process.

To recap, a good recruitment system will convince potential church planters of the benefits of that career choice. Routine, predictable, and professional systems of dealing with candidates will engender confidence in the organization. As more people are trained in the components of the system and the finer details of personal recruiting, the movement has the potential to sustain itself and expand.

FUNDING

In nearly every expanding church planting movement there will come a time when vision for expansion is eclipsed by current resources. While this could be true of a number of systems—recruitment, coaching, and research, for example—it is most keenly felt in the area of funding.

Funding is uniquely wed to ministry. Unfortunately, the axiom is often
accurate that where large sums of money reside there is a dearth of
ministry, and where funding resources are lacking ministry is expanding.
As church planting movements grow, there is a need to expand the
funding base. New movements that plan ahead can avoid expected
pressures before funding realities reach a crisis point.

Funding systems are necessary on both a microcosmic level (the
individual church planter and church plant) and on a macrocosmic level
(the movement as a whole). Relative to the individual church planter,
there are financial needs for personal subsistence, health and disability
insurance, retirement, and continuing education. Procedures to guide
important financial decisions and expectations, such as the creation of a
salary package, are also needed.

Denominations and districts vary widely in what they offer to their
church planters. On one end of the spectrum, there are fully funded
positions which can run for years without interruption. Church planters
appreciate these situations, but when they do exist it is usually evidence
that new church plants are rare within the movement. An overly
comfortable church planter is probably indicative of an under-aggressive
church planting movement. When salary is guaranteed regardless of
productivity, there can be a tendency toward inactivity. As a friend of
mine likes to say, "Fat dogs don't hunt!" On the other end of the
spectrum there are bivocational situations where church planters are
entirely dependent on other employment to supply their needs. Most
church planters wish to avoid purely bivocational positions, but if systems
are in place that bring helpful support in other ways, altruistic church
planters who feel called by God will labor under such circumstances.
Most situations involve a combination of personal, parent church, and
denominational efforts compensate the church planter adequately. This
likely is true even of districts or denominations that can supply full salary
packages should they move toward expansion and greater productivity.

Denominations and districts should create a salary package for church
planters, even if such a package is hypothetical and will not be realized.
If the district, denomination or parent church is inexperienced in hiring
personnel, a standardized salary package mechanism should be in place
to delineate salary, housing allowance, retirement, vacation, health insurance, and other benefits. Some more ecclesiastical denominations
already have a routine process based on experience and education. If
such a formula does not exist, the procedure becomes haphazard and can
lead to feelings of jealousy and irrational thinking. I have typically
indexed church planter salaries to local teachers' salaries, plus ten
percent. By taking the guesswork out of salary structuring energy can be
redirected to more productive pursuits.

When church planters are expected to raise all or part of a salary package from churches, personal friends, and contacts, a number of subsystems need to be in place. For one, most people do not enjoy raising support, so it is the job of district leadership (perhaps through its coaching team) to keep the planter encouraged and accountable for this important aspect of the job. One church planting coach tells his planters, "Work as hard at fund-raising as you think you'll work at evangelism when your new church starts." In newer movements, there is a positive sentiment among district churches to support the new venture. However, as the movement expands and church planting is no longer a novelty, the season of sentiment passes. Some of that sentiment can be recaptured when a new church is particularly unique, such as with a different cultural group.

There are some minor implications for church planters and their finances as it relates to smaller towns and rural areas. The most obvious is that while bivocational church planters might not be noticed as peculiar in a larger communities, they certainly will be noticed in smaller ones. The upside, as with all bivocational church planters in any community, is that there are natural entry points into people's lives, because outside work will normally force relationships to occur. The downside, in a smaller community, is that many people will not consider the new minister and the new church to be as legitimate as the other churches in town. The entire operation may be viewed as a small, struggling entity, unlike established ministers and churches. This is by no mean destiny. Many bivocational church planters do very successful work in smaller communities. One church planter I know is committed to bivocational work even though his church can pay a full salary. He will always work at least eight hours per week outside his church because of the relational advantage it gives him.

On the regional level, church planting movements need to expand their funding base in order to build a growing infrastructure to sustain and expand the work. There will be growing personnel needs and financial pressures to assist church planters and their new churches. Fund-raising for district church planting movements is varied. "Solicitations" refers to general appeals for financial help, either through churches, individuals, or corporate sponsors, and can include annual fundraising drives, church dues, banquets, golf events, bequests, and the like. Fees for services can include percentage charges for receipting and accounting services, taxes on accounts to offset health insurance premiums, or costs for attendance at required events. Finally, there should be clear expectations regarding how and when the new church becomes a financial contributor back to the district or denomination.

Each district or denomination needs to plan accordingly and make sound decisions for its financial future. It may be worthwhile to forge relationships with fund-raising consultants who are experienced in this arena. Even if funding concerns seem remote at the beginning stages of a movement, church planting movements want to avoid the day when vision is eclipsed by available resources.

ASSESSMENT

Care must be exercised in determining who will be assessed. District leaders will be tempted to move recruits quickly from the recruitment phase to assessment, but without background checks, this can be treacherous and costly. It is best if background work is not performed by leaders who have predetermined the suitability of a given candidate. Early on leaders cannot be counted on to be entirely objective in their analysis of candidates since there is a strong underlying agenda to approve people to get the mission underway. However, most leaders know someone who has some personnel experience who can distance themselves emotionally from the decision to move ahead with assessment. Telephone calls to references and secondary references can yield helpful information about church planting proficiency and character. It is also worthwhile, with the candidate's permission, to obtain criminal background information from law enforcement agencies at minimal expense. This necessary intermediary step can save movement leaders countless hours of headaches and thousands of dollars in assessment costs should disqualifying information come to light during the reference and background work.

At the front end of an emerging movement, it may be required to farm out assessment responsibilities to others who have developed proficiency in determining who should plant churches. A number of denominations and parachurch ministries offer something akin to an Assessment Center. District church planting representatives who are sent to Assessment Centers as observers can gain valuable experience to contribute to the movement at large. Over time, they can develop an Assessment Center of their own. The same can be said of the Behavioral Interview process. Currently good materials exist for the training of interviewers, including *Training for Selection Interviewing* (available through ChurchSmart Resources, St. Charles, Ill.), a manual with accompanying videotapes. Occasionally, workshops are offered to refine interviewer skills. Virtually every church planting movement has access to volunteers or other staffers in their region who would perform well and enjoy contributing to the mission as interviewers.

Objective assessment is a given in any church planting movement, and the criteria set forth by those experienced in church planting success indicators should be respected and adhered to. Having said that, I repeat what was stated earlier: the bar can be lowered for those who will plant churches in smaller markets, and assessors should be alerted to the fact that some candidates who would be disqualified or considered marginal for church planting in a larger market might fit perfectly in an area with a smaller population. Notice that my contention is that the bar can be lowered, not eliminated. There are minimal acceptable standards. My experience is that some with solid potential have been inadvisedly disqualified from the church planting arena because assessors did not make allowance for the type of community the candidates might pursue.

This leads to one final component of assessment: venue and timeline considerations. Reference was made earlier to performing a Risk Factor Analysis, which appears as appendix 1. Once a candidate is considered to have a possible future in church planting, movement leaders must determine what other risks enter into the formula. Factors such as cultural fit, proximity to churches who can and will help, preexisting contacts, and proximity to family or natural support groups all contribute to the level of risk that a candidate or candidate couple might be asked to absorb. When leaders work with a candidate through a risk assessment analysis particular attention should be given to any candidate who has some background in a smaller town or rural area. Just because a person has a small town background does not necessarily mean that he or she should be assigned to a similar community, but it may mean that some cultural issues are already settled, which would reduce risk. This tool has been very effective in gauging risk in Wisconsin, and leaders from other movements may find benefit in using this as a template as they develop their own tool. Other factors may emerge, depending on the characteristics of the denomination and region of the country.

On occasion, leaders responsible for placing church planting candidates will recommend (or, if polity allows, assign) a planter to a smaller community that the candidate finds less than desirable. Because some planters might consider a small town as a demotion from a suburban or urban environment, this can be a sensitive pursuit. Nevertheless, wisdom must prevail, and I have encountered this on several occasions. I have learned to use several phrases to put the decision in proper context. I have asked, "Would you rather plant a church of seventy-five people in a desirable community or one of two hundred people in a place without all of the bells and whistles you've come to expect?" I point to the evidence to augment my point. I also tell candidates to pray about the decision, and I say, "From where I stand, I have an opportunity to have you like me now and hate me later, or dislike me now and love me later. Because I have a need to be liked, I'm going to push you toward the smaller town." Finally, I have soothed some reticent church planters with the reminder that planting a church in a smaller town does not mean that they'll necessarily be there forever. It may be that after four or five years of experience and success they will be better outfitted for a larger community more in line with their preferences.

TRAINING

The training of approved church planters is another vital system in any church planting movement. A training system begins with the initial training of church planters. As with assessment systems, at the front end of a church planting movement some training may be farmed out to those who specialize in preparing church planters. Organizations such as ChurchSmart Resources (St. Charles, Ill.), The Church Multiplication Training Center (Colorado Springs, Colo.), New Church Specialties (Kansas City, Mo.), Dynamic Church Planting International (Oceanside, Calif.), and 4:36 Ministries (Lindenhurst, Ill.) have noted proficiency in this type of ministry. Many denominations offer similar programs, and often these are open to outsiders. The important thing is that church planters be given some sort of initiatory training to jump-start their work.

Training should also include occasional in-service and networking opportunities for planters. Movement leadership must be inventive and come up with ways to bring their church planters in touch with other colleagues. Even a small, emerging movement can host an annual church planting retreat, bringing together planting couples, coaches, and other key people. Held at a nice facility in a nice location, such events can be catalytic in forging an immutable bond with others and with the mission. As a movement matures there may be specific training and networking events for those who find themselves planting in small towns or rural environments.

Training should also include access to resources. Books, tapes, videos, and other media should be made available to church planters at the movement's expense. Denominations can also provide scholarships for church planters so they can access other helpful training events, such as those provided by some megachurches. The advent of the Internet gives planters access to other resources germane to the planting of new churches. One subscription service, Bob Logan's CoachNet® (www.coachnet.org), brings together teaching, course training, coaching, networking, and forums specifically related to new works. Such resources demonstrate a cutting-edge approach to ministry expansion by providing forums and resources specifically for the smaller market church planter.

Chapter 10: You Can Do It! (A Case Study)

When leaders who are responsible for regional church planting agree to embrace a systems approach to their mission, they must decide where to begin. Starting a church planting movement is hard, but the work is easier when a measured and intentional strategy is employed.

SYSTEM PRIORITIZATION, IMPLEMENTATION, AND SUMMARY OBSERVATIONS

In situations where some systems are already in place, the challenge for leaders is to eliminate, modify and improve where necessary–and add missing systems as time goes on. In new or "emerging" movements, the task for leaders is to implement whatever systems they can in an orderly and logical fashion. My recommendations come from considerable experience in helping new church planting movements get started, and they come from a certain defendable bias which understands the value of church planting in smaller communities. I prioritize the seven necessary systems in the same order that I listed them in chapter 9.

CHURCH PLANTING SYSTEMS, IN ORDER OF PRIORITY
1. Spiritual dynamics
2. Established church involvement
3. Coaching
4. Recruitment
5. Funding
6. Assessment
7. Training

In a moment you'll see that the backbone of a movement is apostolic leadership that rises up from the coalitions of established church leaders (LEAD Teams) and the coaches that are developed to help church planters succeed. If a denomination requires the involvement of a district church planting or missions committee, I would use that committee to make policy and to grant permission, but I would try to keep implemen-

tation of the movement at the practitioner level. If such an oversight
board does not exist, there is no need to rush into the creation of one.
In general, it takes at least two years for a semblance of a "movement" to
emerge. Leaders must demonstrate patience and not be overly anxious to
mobilize planters too soon. What follows is a fictional compilation of
dozens of encounters I've had with denominational leaders who desper-
ately wanted to see churches planted in their region.

A CASE STUDY

The phone rang, and though the voice on the other end was new, the
content of the call was familiar. "I'm a district superintendent, overseeing
sixty-five churches in our area. I've been to enough church planting
seminars to turn blue in the face, and I've got a nice collection of three-
ring binders. We've tried to plant some new churches, but it's been hard.
We've had some shipwrecks, and we've had to lick some wounds. But I
know that new churches need to be planted. Can you help?"

My heart goes out to these leaders. They sincerely want to serve God
and advance His purposes. They long to hear the stories of changed lives
that come from the planting of new churches, and they want to harness
the power of their established churches. But their church planting self-
esteem is so low that they don't think it will ever happen. As an old
friend of mine describes such a person: "His face was so long that he
could have sucked marbles out of a gopher hole."

My answer to his question? "Yes." I knew that help was available and
that his district could make progress because I'd seen it happen so many
times. "Tell me about your situation. How long have you been on the
job? Tell me about your recent church planting track record."

"I've been the district superintendent for five years now. I think our
district has been typical of many in our denomination. We have some
loyal churches, but we lose one now and then to a natural death. And,
between you and me, there are some that we probably should lose.
They're not expanding the kingdom at all. So a few years ago I spoke to
our Outreach Committee about maybe trying to start some new churches.
Some thought that we should focus on helping our established churches
get better—and then to start planting churches. But most of us agreed
that it would bring some new life into our group if we could get
something going sooner rather than later."

"What did you do?" I asked. "How did you get started?"

"Well, we had a talented pastor who was looking for a change, and
when he heard that we wanted to start a new church he approached me.
He had a friend in another part of the country who had planted a church
which had gone well. We did have some budget money for it, and he was

interested, so we agreed to send him to a suburban environment where we didn't have any churches. They started a Bible study and then had services at a hotel conference room, but it just went nowhere. So it closed less than two years into it, and now I'm not sure what to do. Our district is still supportive, I think, but I did lose some poker chips when that one fell through."

How did we help the superintendent? "Let's get together . . . how about at my office?" So we set up an appointment.

It wasn't that hard to figure out what went wrong. The positive sentiment to do something good for God and his kingdom overshadowed sound thinking and experience. It was like a mild version of the story of Jephthah in Judges 11. He wanted victory so badly that he told God he would sacrifice the first living creature to come out of his home. That foolish pledge resulted in the sacrifice of his daughter. Zeal for a cause without a solid foundation can yield bitter results. "I want to encourage you," I told the superintendent. "We'll get you there, and it will take some time, but it won't take that much time. My concern right now is not that you plant some churches but that you build a movement."

We talked through their present situation and their available resources. I described the various phases of the development of a church planting movement (as described in chapter 8). This group had a disappointment with a failed church plant, but their corporate vision had not evaporated. There was still some positive sentiment to build on, and the superintendent still had the trust of his constituents. I learned a few other things. He felt good about a number of leaders in his district. There were some good, solid churches and some good energy to capitalize on. He did not have a lot of obstacles to overcome; he just wanted to lead well so they could build momentum.

"I have a strategy in mind for you," I said. I began to explain the difference between an event and a movement. "A movement will outlive the initial visionaries. It's not personality-dependent. Systems are in place—there are routine, reliable procedures that, when followed, will result in success. God's Word is full of examples where organization took precedence over personalities. So we'll try to build an organization that keeps on giving." I showed him a chart to explain how he could build a team, implement systems, and create the necessary momentum to have a multiplying church planting movement. I told him that he would have to have the patience to see this through, because we really wouldn't be starting a new church until the second year. But the payoff would be exciting. They would avoid repeating the mistakes of the past, and they really would be advancing God's work.

TEMPLATE FOR STARTING A DISTRICT-WIDE CHURCH PLANTING MOVEMENT

YEAR	OBJECTIVE	SYSTEM
Year 1	Start a movement of prayer	Spiritual Dynamics
	Develop a team of pastors and key lay leaders (LEAD Team) who will champion and implement church planting in the district.	Etablished church involvement
	Begin training of church planting coaches.	Coaching
	Begin recruitment strategy.	Recruitment
	Identify "head coach."	
Year 2	Install head coach and maintain Year 1 systems.	
	Recruit one or two church planters.	Recruitment
	Start funding strategy.	Funding
	Develop assessment strategy, and properly assess recruits.	Assessment
	Mobilize and coach at least one new church planter, and expose him to an initial training event.	Coaching, Training
	Identify potential leaders to form new LEAD Teams.	
Year 3	Start second LEAD Team in district.	Established church involvement
	Plant 2-4 new churches.	
	Monitor systems toward maturity.	

"Your denomination has a rich history of dependence on God. I'm sure you have people in your circle who are intercessors and understand spiritual warfare. How can you capitalize on this resource? At the front end of this movement I'd like to see some sort of intentional prayer strategy. And I don't just mean putting a prayer blurb in the monthly communique; I mean, let's find those who pray and are willing to pray for new churches to start." We brainstormed some ideas. "Let's set up another meeting, about a month from now. You can buy me lunch. In the meantime I have two assignments. First, think through and start implementing something on **spiritual dynamics**. I want you to tell me who is doing what and how you are communicating with those who will pray. Second, I want you to start thinking about pastors and key lay leaders in your district who will help to support you strategically. Can you bring me a list of eight to ten leaders, mostly pastors, who have the clout to help see a movement get off the ground? After we get something going with spiritual dynamics I want to make sure that we have **established church involvement** to get us on a solid foundation." We set up the next month's appointment and we closed our time in prayer.

I e-mailed my superintendent friend a couple of weeks out, and I asked him how it was coming together. He told me that he had already enlisted nearly twenty people just to pray for church planting. They would be linked with a biweekly e-mail that would come from the district office. Good. I asked to be put on the list so I could see what was going out to intercessors. And besides, I'd even pray from time to time. What else? "Well, I am starting to put a blurb in the monthly district newsletter, asking for prayer. But I'm also asking that pastors let me know about some potential intercessors. I'm calling this our Heaven's Angels Team. I thought that was kind of cute." Fine. It would work.

We met for lunch, and the superintendent was pleased that some people were already praying. They had a dedicated e-mail address at the office just for intercession, and someone was working toward putting prayer needs on their web page. "Great!" I said. "Now let's talk about **established church involvement**. Who do you have in mind that we could recruit to be on a strategy team? I'm wanting to get these folks together every other month or so for an overnight session we'll call a LEAD meeting. That stands for the four things we'll try to do together: Learn, Encourage, Achieve, and Dream." I couldn't tell if he was impressed with my acronym, but he did give it some thought. The super-intendent told me about their district Outreach Committee, but I really wanted to focus not so much on an administrative board but rather on those who really could marshal some resources. I wanted leaders who might say they didn't have time to be on our strategy team. "Let's go over your list." He had some good people, but his main concern was that it might be hard to get some of them on board due to time commitments. "Could you get most of these folks to a free lunch?" I asked. "If we could get them to join us for ninety minutes, and you fed them well, I would explain what happens when we combine relationships worth building with a mission worth chasing. We're out to build a team." He agreed to work on my suggestions, and we closed in prayer.

Included in the biweekly e-mail prayer notice that week was a request to pray for the development of a team, a LEAD Team, that would help to jump-start church planting in the district. I was pleased to see that. We traded e-mail that put together the final details for our lunch with the other district leaders. I learned that he had received eight positive responses from those he was enlisting, with a possible ninth planning on attending the meeting.

A few weeks later we gathered in a decent restaurant at a central location. They had a side room reserved for us. The superintendent had eight pastors with him, and they seemed like a good bunch. After the pleasantries of introductions, and following the meal, I took the floor to explain what we were trying to accomplish. We wanted to start a LEAD Team that would provide the primary vision for the new district church planting mission. I explained that we would try to meet at least five times each year, and that we would for the most part be together for twenty-four hours. Besides learning about church planting and plotting a future, we'd do some fun things together. We'd stay at a nice place, we'd share our lives, pray for each other. And we'd do fun stuff together . . . like golfing, or horseback riding, or paintball. "I'd urge you to come to just one LEAD meeting. My experience is that even if you're already overbooked, once you're part of this you won't want to miss it. Most pastors tell me that they haven't had friendships develop like this in ministry—ever. And they say it's great to be part of something that really accomplishes a mission. And . . . it's at district expense. You just show up and they'll pick up the tab." The superintendent managed to force a generous smile while he did the mental calculations. Later I told him, "Don't worry. This will be the best money you'll ever spend. These are the very people who will be fueling your movement anyway." Everyone agreed to come.

So we were off and running. The first meeting had to be at a nice place to set the pace for the future. It was winter, and we went to a resort with an indoor water park—a place not many pastors would normally go to. It would seem extravagant, in a good way. Everyone arrived by 1 p.m., and we spent the first hour giving rudimentary intro- ductions, painting a picture again of what we wanted to be. We spent a few minutes looking at a videotape about church planting, and we discussed the implications, closing in prayer. That was our "learning" component of the meeting. By 3 p.m. we were in the water park, hitting the slides, playing basketball. I'd seen the process again and again. They always start out with hesitation, thinking, "Is this something we can do?" But even the most reserved reverends eventually find themselves loosening up and enjoying the time. At night we had a nice dinner out, and we concluded the evening by gathering in groups of three and four to pray for each of our own personal needs. I always prescribe laying hands on each other for prayer. It builds a level of depth and camaraderie while conveying the power of God into participants' lives. After prayer, some of them went back to the water park or hot tub, and others just hung out and chatted. Most of the day was comprised of the second component of our meeting, Encouragement.

The next morning, after breakfast, the real "work" began. We talked more about church planting and assigned everyone the task of looking into a community or two in their area that could use a new church. That was the Achieving part. Finally, for our Dreaming, we spread maps out and prayed for the Lord to lead. The meeting concluded by noon, and we were on our way home.

I've led a lot of meetings like this. Remember, the idea is to combine mission and relationship: "relationships worth building and dreams worth chasing." By themselves these often go nowhere, but together they form a potent weapon. One friend of mine attended his first LEAD meeting and by bedtime had figured out that not much real "work" had been accomplished. It was mostly just fun and prayer up until then. He complained mildly to the head coach that the meeting could be structured more efficiently. The head coach told him, "You're concerned about running a meeting, but I'm concerned about building a movement. Just watch and see what happens." This friend of mine did see what happened, and he now serves as a head coach, too.

This LEAD Team became the foundation of the superintendent's church planting movement in his district. There was one hundred percent buy-in. Each participant in the first meeting signed on to be part of it for the foreseeable future. The superintendent needed to hold team members accountable for the assignments they had agreed to. He needed to e-mail them and call them from time to time, until their next meeting which was held two months later. But we all know what happens with district superintendents. Theirs is a tough job. It is very time-intensive, and it is hard for them to function well in the "non-urgent important" part of life. I needed to keep my eye out for someone from the group who could serve as head coach.

We kept functioning as a LEAD Team in the months that followed. We kept everyone busy with assignments, and we slowly created church planting systems. One system to develop was **coaching**. Some participants took the role of church planting coaches, and that required some training, particularly from the *Church Planters' Toolkit*. We had these coaches show up two hours early for LEAD meetings to go over the materials and practice coaching skills. Two team members had a passion for **recruiting**. They had people in their churches that put together a web site, developed a logo, and created materials that outlined the procedures and highlighted the advantages that this new church planting movement would offer potential planters. They started to gather materials that others were using, and they gleaned good ideas to implement themselves. Right then we weren't actively looking for planters, but we wanted to be ready to recruit well when the time came.

It's possible to do more than what we did in a year, but in my experience it takes about that long to get a team functioning well enough to implement a few church planting systems. The team will grow, too, because at each meeting we'll ask, "Who else do we want here?" And there will be some fallout, with some members moving away or some slipping away through natural entropy. Generally, a team works best when there are around eight to ten participants.

"How do you think it's going, now that we've been at it a year?" I asked the district superintendent. He was pleased, but a little anxious, too. It was heartening to see a team develop. Many now had their churches contributing financially, and a solid prayer team had developed. We had had five LEAD meetings in some pretty memorable locations, with a lot of laughs shared. But he was feeling some internal and external pressure to produce a church. "I keep wondering when and how the Lord will give us our first church planter," he confided. I encouraged him, "We probably could have started a church by now, but I'd rather that we're health-driven and not calendar-driven. Now, with year two underway we'll get serious about getting a new work on the map. And it should be a good one." We reviewed what had been accomplished, and actually the list was pretty impressive. We had systems in place for four of our seven priorities. Not all systems were entirely mature yet, but they were on their way. I had one other suggestion for the superintendent, having to do with one of the team members who was particularly responsive to all we were doing. "I think he'd make a great head coach. Why don't I try to work through him rather than through you? You can still be a participant, but let's empower others to own this movement." He agreed, and we now had a head coach.

At our next meeting, the transfer of leadership to a head coach went well. The superintendent didn't attend every meeting after that. In fact, the entire team could feel a deepened sense of ownership because now it was apparent that their loyalty was to the cause rather than just to the superintendent. I did an overview of where we had been and where we were going. "We now have enough structure to warrant planting a church or two, so I want us to be on the lookout for potential church planters." Those who were engineering the recruitment strategy unveiled some of their work. They had a decent web site just ready to launch. An attractive folder with some good information about the area and the movement was presented. There was a "road map" to help explain to aspiring church planters how they could get involved. "If someone didn't know any better, they would figure that this district could plant churches!" I said. And I had a suggestion. "Let's get a letter out to all of our district pastors and key lay people to ask them to scout for us. They can be on the lookout for entrepreneurial self-starters who have a calling toward mission. We've got to have some potential church planters around here. And we'll explain how we have been working to provide the structure and support necessary so our next planter will have the best shot at success."

The good news was that they still had some money in the district coffers that had been earmarked for church planting. The reality, however, was that now was a good time to start thinking about funding issues. Team members felt that district churches would support a new church planter when he was endorsed, and that the failure of a couple of years ago wouldn't have too much of a residual effect. Three of the members took responsibility to come up with a plan for long-term financial stability. Eventually they did present some ideas to the group, some of which were project-oriented (such as a golf tournament) and some of which were more systematic (such as requiring new churches to tithe from their offerings back to the district church planting fund). There was also a district-wide "Seed Money Offering" to coincide with Thanksgiving later that year. Team members worked on promotional materials and a video, and the project was well received.

By the next LEAD meeting, there was good news. At least three potential church planters had been located. Two were hits on the web site, and one was a seasoned youth pastor couple from one of the district churches. The web site contacts were long shots because they were from other parts of the country, and they were from different denominational backgrounds. But they were worthy of follow-up. The youth pastor couple had been referred by their senior pastor, who was responding to the district-wide mailing. We invited them to the LEAD meeting. I had at one time told the team that former youth pastors can be good church planters because "they like to do crazy things, but now they want to do them with adults!" We learned of their dreams and shared the positives about planting a church—especially when there were support mechanisms in place. We prayed for the couple that they would know the leading of the Lord. If they were interested in pursuing church planting we would send them to an Assessment Center. Our head coach said, "Our job isn't to talk you into something you shouldn't do. But if you're cut out for church planting, let's get you into the game." I was proud of him.

With a potential church planting couple on the horizon we needed to get serious about a location. In fact, the couple had already asked in countless ways, "Where are you targeting? Where is the need the greatest?" My response was typical. "Everywhere! But the issue isn't so much where the greatest needs are; the issue is where can we give you the best chance to win. For all of us—you, the district, the kingdom—we need to make this next church plant a win."

This is where my experience—and admittedly, my bias—rings through clearly. With the team members we had looked at a number of potential church planting sites, keeping in mind the risk factors involved (appendix 1). My recommendation was that as long as risk factors could be reduced sufficiently we should look at a small town. "It's easier to win there. And if we get some wins under our belt, the small towns will pave the way for the bigger markets. It's what Wal-Mart does, by the way."

The couple eventually attended an Assessment Center, hosted by a sister denomination. Two of our LEAD Team members attended as assessors, and that helped to whet their appetite for creating an **assessment** system, eventually, for this movement. But right now it was sufficient to watch others do it and to learn from them. Our potential planters came back enthusiastically approved, and they learned an incredible amount about themselves and church planting. So did our team members. Their participation in the Assessment Center only helped to legitimize everything we had wanted them to learn from the beginning.

Over the course of that second year the new church plant began to fall into place. The most important factor that helped to frame our action plan was that the church where the youth pastor had been serving became enthusiastic about the idea. That helped to make a lot of things easier. "If we can plant a church within striking distance of this home church . . . especially in a small town . . . we will have eliminated a lot of risk for this couple," I reminded the team. "It gives them an emotional support base, it covers some of the funding issues, and it gives them a running start with potential core group members and ministry partners." As a matter of fact, the parent church became so passionate about the project that the senior pastor encouraged the planters to use their youth group to do some of the preliminary research in area communities. They did demographic studies, and door-to-door visitation, and attended community churches. Eventually a place was settled on. It was a town of around 8,000 people, about 25 miles from the parent church.

All of the usual systems then clicked into gear. The church planting couple was paraded around the district to raise financial support. Much of it came from parent church support and a special gift from a wealthy benefactor. They attended a church planting "boot camp" for an initial **training** event. And they were coached by two of our LEAD Team members who had learned the art of **coaching** and the specifics of church planting over the previous months. The monthly meetings and routine phone calls helped the couple to feel affirmed, and the guidance offered helped them avoid many costly errors.

The church eventually launched with great success. If it had been in a large community it might not have been noticed, but in this smaller community it made quite a splash. It was the most "happening" church around, quickly becoming a bona fide player in the religious life of the community. And many people came to Christ—people who didn't know that church could be so fun and relevant. One new convert shared her testimony at the district annual meeting, receiving a standing ovation as she thanked those who cared enough to start a new church for people like her.

And the movement itself began to grow. Systems became mature, and momentum picked up. Recruiting wasn't as hard as they had imagined it would be. Not all who applied were accepted and approved—a sure sign that the systems were working. In the days to come more LEAD Teams developed and the church planting vision expanded beyond all that they "could ask or imagine" (Col. 3:20, NIV). There were some failures, of course, but the momentum was strong enough to overcome the negative inertia. And with a solid track record, the movement went after the larger communities and urban centers.

In time I drew closure to my consulting relationship with this district, and I had the superintendent take me out for lunch for our final debrief. Maybe it all hadn't gone as wonderfully as my chart said it would. It always looks better in the books than it does in real life. But an extraordinary amount of progress had been made in a relatively short amount of time. This district would be successfully planting many churches in the months and years to come. "Thanks for your help!" he said sincerely. I reminded him of how well things can go when we start small.

APPENDIX 1

CHURCH PLANTING MOBILIZATION
RISK FACTOR ANALYSIS

Church planter_____ Date _____

Church planting is a risky business, but experience shows that when a qualified church planter is fitted with the right environmental situation the likelihood of success is greatly enhanced. The following guide is to help you, the potential church planter, determine whether now is the right time and this is the right place for you to enter into the arena of church planting.

For the following, circle the number on each line which best represents your situation:

How will you be personally funded?

1----------2----------3----------4----------5
faith   bi-vocational   partial support   spouse/   fully funded
                                                     strong support

Does the site selection match your cultural background or experience?

1----------2----------3----------4----------5
not really   a little   moderately   pretty much   absolutely

How many ministry partners will move with you?

1----------2----------3----------4----------5
none   1 or 2   3 or 4   5 or 6   7 or 8

How many pre-existing adult contacts (individuals or couples), that you already know or are aware of, might likely become part of your team?

1————————2————————3————————4————————5
none   1 or 2   3 or 4   5 or 6   7 or 8

How near is your family or your spouse's family or natural support group?

1————————————2————————————3
would take an airplane   within driving distance   nearby
                          for a weekend visit.

How closely does your ministry site approximate your geographic roots?

1————————————2————————————3
not much   somewhat   quite a bit

How close are you to other supportive churches who really want you to succeed?

1————————————2————————————3
not close at all   somewhat   very close

How much vocational ministry success have you personally experienced?

1————————————2————————————3
none so far   a little   a lot

Scoring

Now total your score, and compare it to the general guidelines below.

8-15 HIGH RISK: As a qualified church planter you will seriously need to consider whether this is the right time and/or the right place to church plant. Prayerfully discuss this with district personnel who may be able to point you to less risky opportunities or help you to re-engineer your time line.

16-23 MODERATE RISK: As a qualified church planter, you need to realize that this will be a challenging experience. Bring this decision before the Lord and others experienced in church planting. If Godís calling seems clear, proceed with conviction and wisdom. If there is strong uncertainty, district personnel may be able to point you to less risky opportunities or help you to re-engineer your time line. Remember: some risk is normal. The Great Commission does not call us to avoid challenging situations!

24-32 LOW RISK: As a qualified church planter, the environmental issues here seem to point toward a positive church planting experience. There will still be challenges, of course. You must prayerfully consider God's leading in this venture. If he so leads, you will likely find success.

My numerical score _____

My risk category _____

Other thought and/or action steps:

APPENDIX 2

SNEAK PREVIEW SYSTEMS
Tom Nebel

	Phase 1	Phase 2	Phase 3	Phase 4
"OLD WAY"	Pre-Natal, Launch Team Development	Preparatory Worship, Perhaps 6-9 Months, Continued Launch, Team Development	Launch: Go Public	
"NEW WAY"	Pre-Natal, Launch Team, Development	Preview Services, Continued Launch, Team Development	Preparatory Worship, 4-6 Weeks	Launch: Go Public

In the "Old Way" of doing things, the church planter would, after amassing 20 committed adults, begin "Preparatory Worship" on Sunday mornings. The advantage was that it helped launch team members actually feel like a church was starting, and it gave them something to do on Sunday mornings. Slowly but surely we could build a larger launch team, working toward a critical mass of 40 adults, which would lead us toward launch. The disadvantage is that once preparatory worship began, so much of the church planters energies were invested in the Sunday experience, and much of the other developmental issues (evangelism, leadership development) suffered.

In the "New Way" of doing things, preparatory worship is reduced to a small period of time, perhaps 4-6 weeks prior Launch: Go Publicto the actual launch of the church. But, in order to gather momentum, help launch team members feel like church is happening, and to showcase to potential launch team members, "Sneak Preview" services occur approximately every six weeks. They are advertised through: word of mouth, personal written invitations, radio, direct mail, newspaper inserts, and so on. During the Preview Service phase, services are followed by information meetings and other "in-gathering" events or appointments to help those who have attended a service and were favorably impacted to make a commitment to the launch team. Sneak Preview services can occur any time during the week: Sunday morning, Sunday evening, Saturday evening, etc.. And they can be done virtually any time during the calendar year.

Advantages include:
❑ Less burnout on the planter, who can give more attention to strengthening the base of the church.
❑ Higher quality of service, because quality of the event is not diluted by every week drudgery.
❑ Lower rent costs prior to launch, since facilities are not necessarily used every week.
❑ Preview Services can be performed by a very small group of people, as long as they are borrowing personnel from other places.
❑ The willingness of other talented individuals and churches to help on occasion is vastly increased.
❑ If the planter s primary giftedness is in the area of preaching, he is allowed to showcase his abilities much sooner in the process, building momentum and confidence in the leader.
❑ One advantage to the denomination, district, or church planting movement is that this format allows other churches in the denomination to help out on occasion, which builds a sense of camaraderie and legitimizes the planting of new churches.
❑ Preview Services can serve as a baby-step for established churches who may have a possible interest in planting daughter churches by test-marketing the viability and interest for a new church in a neighboring community or geographical location.
❑ There will be an increased level of excitement for Launch Team members, as they see the theoretical vision of the planter become real.

Disadvantages/Implications
❑ Planter will need to budget for higher advertising expenses at the front end of the plant.
❑ It is recommended that planters with high skill levels and experience budget more heavily on the first few services, and rely on word-of-mouth after that.
❑ It is recommended that planters with emerging skills and experience begin slowly and then advertise heavily when minimum levels of proficiency are attained.

---

[2]Ibid.